What grandma used to cook

Translation by Annette and Brian Solomon
© 1996 by NK-DRUCK Verlag und Offsetdruckerei GmbH,
In der Klotzbach 14, D-57290 Neunkirchen (Germany),
Phone (+49) 27 35 78 43 0, Fax (+49) 27 35 78 43 22
All rights reserved. No part of this book may be
reproduced in any form or by any electronic or mechanical
means, including information storage and retrieval devices
or systems, without prior written permission from the
publisher.
Printed in Germany by NK-DRUCK.
ISBN 3-9803491-4-4

**You are interested
in a Volume II of these
recipes?
Please mail to the publisher
NK-DRUCK!**

Eine Hausfrau steht an jedem Tage
immer vor der gleichen Frage.
Sagt mir nur: „Was koch ich heute,
bekömmlich und schmackhaft, für meine Leute?"
Vieles kommt da in Betracht,
daß sie es auch richtig macht!
Welche Vorräte bieten Garten und Haus?
Wie sieht's mit den Vitaminen aus?
Reste von gestern, gab es die nicht?
Bei zu vielen Kalorien steigt das Gewicht!
Was habe ich im Angebot gelesen,
wäre das nicht passend für heute gewesen?
Am Abend rechnet sie mit Gästen!
Was paßt am besten zu größeren Festen?
Ein Blick zur Uhr! Ob das Geld wohl reicht?
Das Rechte zu wählen ist gar nicht so leicht.

Da bietet sich ein Kochbuch an,
in dem die Hausfrau blättern kann.
Der Küchenzettel ist bald aufgestellt,
Zeit spart sie und vielleicht auch Geld!

Das haben auch Frauen aus Wilnsdorf bedacht,
als sie sich mit Umsicht an's Werk gemacht.

"What do I cook today, wholesome and nice?"
So much to choose from, perfection has its price.
What do garden and larder have to offer?
Nutrients and minerals, vital even to the greatest scoffer.

Yesterdays leftovers. That I could use.
Too many joules! Tis difficult to choose.
A special offer to buy and prepare.
Guests coming by. Which meal shall we share?

A look at the clock. How time flies.
My purse is empty. Now, what shall I buy?
Making the right choice, that is the question,
especially when housewives strive for perfection.

A cookbook! Now, thats what I need.
Putting a menue together, easy indeed.
Not only a time-saver. No, more Id say!
Also easy on the budget. Twill take me a long way".

Women from a small village in Germany realized this too.
Sitting together, they knew what to do.

Ein Kochbuch, das war unser Ziel,
wir schrieben auf und sammelten viel.
Wir haben Rezepte ausprobiert
und schließlich gewählt und gut sortiert.
Nicht unbekannt ist uns dabei geblieben,
daß manches Buch bereits von Hand geschrieben,
doch wollen wir es trotzdem wagen
und möchten zuversichtlich sagen:
Ein neues Kochbuch, ein gutes Gericht
bringt jeder Hausfrau ein freundlich Gesicht.
Wenn unser Buch so Anklang gefunden
und wenn die erste Scheu überwunden,
fangen die Kinder und auch der Mann
nach unserm Buch zu kochen an!

Zum Schluß gestattet uns die Bitte:
Nehmt Gott den Herrn in eure Mitte.
Durch seine Gaben überreich gesegnet,
dankt ihm, der freundlich uns begegnet.

"A cookbook! Lets work and prepare".
Getting together, they started to share.

Though the market is flooded with books of all kinds,
they diligently worked and tickled their minds.
To create a cookbook, easy to use,
from which even children and husband
would know what to choose.

In closing, allow us say:
"Honour God, the Lord in your midst, everyday!
Through His gifts given so freely, He blesses and cares,
and lightens your way."

Metric - Imperial Conversions

The imperial ingredient weights have been rounded to 1 oz for each 25 g, and though the proportions of the ingredients in the dishes are identical, the quantities are slightly less in metric amount. It is therefore important to keep to either the metric column or the imperial one exclusively. Do not mix the two systems. The recipes may not work if you do.

Tischgebete – vor dem Essen

Wir falten unsre Hände
vor jedem Bissen Brot
zum Dank, Herr, daß ohn' Ende
du sendest, was uns not.

O Gott, von dir wir alles haben,
wir preisen dich für deine Gaben.
Du speisest uns, weil du uns liebst;
o segne auch, was du uns gibst.

Vater, segne diese Speise,
uns zur Kraft und dir zum Preise.
Laß uns hier in unsrer Zeit
reifen für die Ewigkeit.

Laß uns, Herr, beim Trinken, Essen
deiner Güte nicht vergessen,
teil uns deine Gaben aus,
füll mit Frieden Herz und Haus.

Du bist's, der alles Gute schafft,
du gibst uns Speise und Lebenskraft.
Laß nun, o Gott, auch dir allein
all unser Tun geheiligt sein.

Prayers of Thanksgiving

Now thank we all our God, with hearts and hands and voices,
Who wondrous things hath done, in whom His world rejoices,
Who from our mothers arms hath blessed us on our way
With countless gifts of love, and still is ours today.

***

For health and strength and daily food,
We give you thanks O Lord.

***

We thank Thee, then O Father, for all things bright and good,
The seed-time and the harvest, our life, our health, our food;
Accept the gifts we offer, for all Thy love imparts, and what Thou most desirest,
Our humble, thankful hearts.
All good gifts around us are sent from heaven above;
Then thank the Lord, O thank the Lord for all His Love

***

For what we have received, O Lord, we are truely thankful.

Der Backes und seine Ordnung

In unserem Dorf gab es früher 7 Backhäuser. Sie gehörten Backes-Gemeinschaften mit 12 bis 18 „Erben" (Familien). Ein Mitglied war der „Schulze". Er verwaltete den Schlüssel und bei ihm hing auch die Tafel mit den Namen der Erben und deren Backtag. Nach dieser „Backes-Ordnung" stand jeder Familie „d'r Dag" (ein bestimmter Tag in der Woche) zur Benutzung zu. Die Benutzung war kostenlos, jedoch wurden notwendige Auslagen für die Unterhaltung des Backes auf die Erben umgelegt.

Es durften auch Nachbarn backen, die nicht zu den „Erben" gehörten. Sie konnten allerdings nur backen, wenn der Backes nicht voll ausgenutzt war. Sie mußten eine geringe Gebühr bezahlen (für Schornsteinfeger usw.).

„D'r Dag" wechselte für die Erben nach Neujahr. So kam nicht immer die gleiche Familie am unbeliebten Montag dran. Montags mußte man nämlich mindestens zwei Schanzen mehr zum Anheizen verbrennen, da der Backes sonntags kalt blieb. Zudem war der Montag ja auch der Waschtag!

According to Backes Rules

Our village used to have 7 bakeries in the early days. These were owned by the "Backes Community": 12 to 18 families all told. One of the members was "Schulze". He held the key to the bakeries. A slate, on which the names of the families, called "heirs", and their respective turns (Dr Dag - The Day) for baking were written, hung in his home. According to the "Backes Rules", each family was given a particular day of the week to use the bakery. Use of the bakeries was free of charge. Yet, the total cost of maintenance was divided amoungst the "heirs".

Of course, neighbours, who were not counted as "heirs", were also permitted to use the bakeries. For them, use was only permitted when the bakeries were not being fully used by the "community" members. A low maintenance fee was taken.

"Dr Dag" (The Day) was fixed anew annually after New Years Day. In so-doing, it was assured that no family would continually have its turn on the most disliked Monday. It was on Mondays that far more wood had to be fetched to stoke the ovens. The ovens were not normally heated on Sundays. Moreover, Monday was traditionally "laundry day".

Samstags kam nach dem Brot noch der Sonntagskuchen in den Ofen. Da durften natürlich alle Familien backen. Das konnte bei Kerzenlicht oft bis Mitternacht dauern.

In der Erntezeit trocknete man nach dem Brotbacken die Schnetzeln (Apfelscheiben), Hotzeln (Birnenstücke) und Gwetschen (Pflaumen) über Nacht im Backofen.

Die Backes-Gemeinschaft war wie eine große Familie.

On Saturdays, after the bread, cake for the following Sunday was baked. All families were then permitted to bake. Baking cakes on a Saturday was often done by candle-light through midnight, making use of the "after heat".

During the harvest season, the "after heat" was also used to dry the "Schnetzeln" (apple-rings), "Hotzeln" (pear bits) and "Gwetschen" (prunes) overnight.

The "Backes Community" was like a large family.

Backesbruet

Zutaten: 20 Pfd. Roggenmehl (evtl. 2 oder 3 Pfd. durch Weizenmehl ersetzen)
2 Pfd. Sauerteig
200 g Salz
6 P. frische Hefe
5 l lauwarmes Wasser

Zubereitung:
Roggen- und Weizenmehl mischen. Sauerteig und Hefe mit 5 l lauwarmem Wasser auflösen und mit einem Teil des Mehles im Trog mischen. Einige Stunden (möglichst über Nacht) gehen lassen. Alles gut verkneten mit Zugabe von Salz und wenig Wasser (nasse Hände!). Teig nochmals 1 1/2 Stunden gehen lassen, dann Brote formen und erneut kurz gehen lassen.
Bei 250° (vorgeheizt) in ca. 1 1/2 - 2 Stunden abbacken.

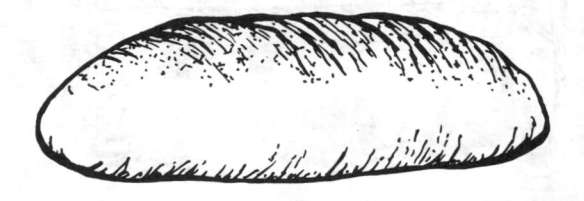

Backes' Leavened bread (Backesbruet)

Ingredients

Metric		Imperial	
10 kg	rye flour	20 lbs	rye flour
(optional 1 - 1.5 kg wheaten flour)		(optional 2-3 lbs wheaten flour)	
2 kg	leaven	4 lbs	leaven
(recipe on following page)			
200 g	salt	8 oz	salt
240 g	compressed yeast	1/2 lb	compressed yeast
5 l	luke-warm water	10 pints	luke-warm water

Method

Mix rye and wheaten flour. Dissolve leaven and yeast in 5 l of water. Mix leaven and yeast mixture well with part of flour and leave over-night. On the following day, blend and knead all ingredients well to a smooth, soft dough, gradually adding salt and water. Leave dough to rise until double its bulk - approx. 90 min. Turn out onto floured surface; knead and shape into loaves. Let rise. Bake in hot oven at 250° C (500° F) for 90 - 120 min.

**When you pray,
four stalks will grow from two grains of corn.**
                                              Don Bosco

***Wenn ihr betet,
wachsen aus zwei Körnern vier Halme.***
                                              Don Bosco

From grandmas Kitchen

(Aus Omas Küche)

Sauerteig

1/8 l warmes Wasser mit soviel Roggenmehl verrühren, daß ein sämiger Brei entsteht. Den Teig zugedeckt 3 Tage warm stehen lassen, bis er gesäuert und von Bläschen durchsetzt ist.
1/8 l Wasser unterrühren und noch einmal soviel Roggenmehl unterrühren, bis ein zäher Teig entsteht.
1 Tag stehen lassen.

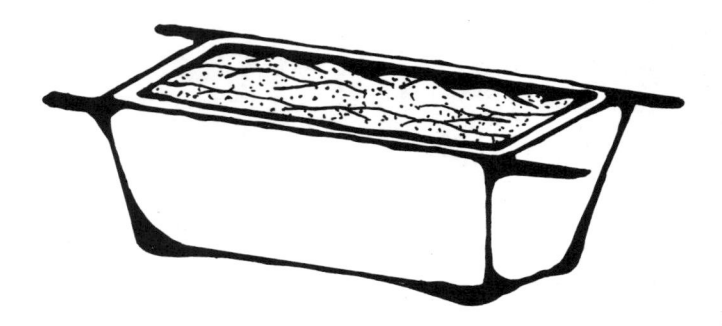

Leaven (Sauerteig)

Mix 125 ml/1/4 pint warm water with enough rye flour to make a creamy paste. Cover and leave paste in a warm place for three days, until it turns sour and becomes frothy.
Add another 125 ml/1/4 pint warm water and mix in the same amount of rye flour to make a sticky dough. Leave covered in a warm place for another day.
Leaven is then ready to use. Refrigerate.

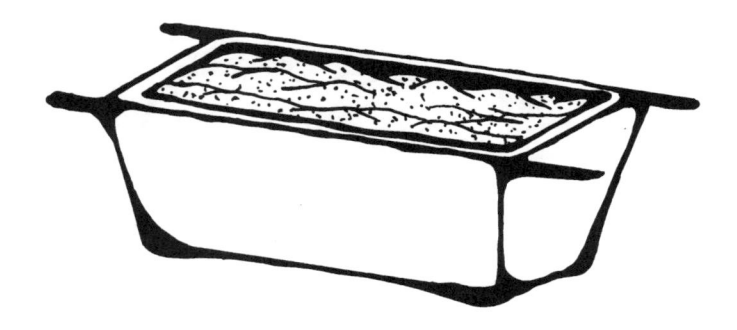

Sijjerlänner Räiweköche

Zutaten:
- 2 Pfd. Mehl
- 2 Eier
- 1 P. Hefe
- 1 EBl. Salz
- 2 Pfd. geriebene rohe Kartoffeln
- 1/4 l Milch

Zubereitung:
Aus den Zutaten einen Hefeteig bereiten und gut gehen lassen. Den Teig in eine große Kastenform füllen und noch einmal gehen lassen.
Im vorgeheizten Ofen bei 220° - 230° 1 - 1 1/2 Std. backen.

Grated potato cake (Sijjerlänner Räiwekoche)

Ingredients

Metric		Imperial	
1 kg	white flour	2 lbs	white flour
2	eggs	2	eggs
1 cake	compressed yeast	1 cake	compressed yeast
1 T	salt	1 T	salt
1 kg	grated potatoes	2 lbs	grated potatoes
250 ml	milk	1/2 pint	milk

Method

Blend all ingredients and knead to a smooth dough. Leave to rise until double its bulk. Then knead again and form into loaf using enough flour to prevent sticking; put in greased loaf tin; let rise once again. Bake at 220° C (425° F) for 60 - 90 min.

Aebbel- on Gwätschekōche

Zutaten:
- 500 g Mehl
- 30 g Hefe
- 1/4 l Milch
- 100 g Zucker
- 100 g Butter
- 1 kg Äpfel oder Pflaumen
- 50 g Korinthen

Zubereitung:

Mehl in eine Schüssel geben, eine Vertiefung hineindrücken, die Hefe hineinbröckeln und mit lauwarmer Milch, etwas Mehl und 1 Teel. Zucker zu einem Vorteig verrühren; ca. 15 Min. aufgehen lassen. Restlichen Zucker, eine Prise Salz und Butter auf dem Rand verteilen, verkneten und den Teig schlagen, bis er Blasen wirft; auf einem gefetteten Backblech ausrollen und aufgehen lassen.

Mürbe Äpfel schälen, entkernen und in Scheiben schneiden. Den Teig damit belegen und mit gewaschenen, gut abgetropften Korinthen bestreuen.

Den Kuchen mit gefettetem Pergamentpapier bedecken, bei 200° etwa 25 Min. backen und noch heiß mit Zucker bestreuen.

Apple or plum cake (Aebbel- / Gwätscheköche)

Ingredients

Metric		Imperial	
500 g	white flour	1 lb	white flour
30 g	compressed yeast	1 1/2 oz	compressed yeast
250 ml	milk	1/2 pint	milk
100 g	sugar	4 oz	sugar
100 g	butter	4 oz	butter
1 kg	apples or plums	2 lbs	apples or plums
50 g	dried currants	2 oz	dried currants

Method

Sift flour into bowl. Dissolve yeast and 1 teaspoon of sugar in a little lukewarm milk. Let stand for 5 - 10 min. Add yeast mixture to flour and blend in all remaining ingredients. Beat vigorously, blending to a smooth dough until air bubbles form. Turn out onto a greased baking pan and roll out. Leave a while to rise. In the meantime, peel apples, remove core and cut into wedges. Spread apple wedges and currants on rolled out dough. Cover with greaseproof paper and bake in a preheated oven (200° C / 400° F) for approximately 25 min. Sprinkle with sugar while still hot.

Krebbelcher

Zutaten für Teig:
- 2 Pfd. Mehl
- 20 g Hefe
- 125 g Zucker
- 1/4 - 3/8 l Milch
- 150 g Butter oder Margarine
- 6 - 8 Eier
- 2 P. Vanillezucker
- 1 Prise Salz

Zum Ausbacken:
- 1 - 2 Pfd. Schweineschmalz, Biskin oder Palmin

Zum Wälzen:
- 1/2 Pfd. Zucker
- 1 - 2 EBl. Zimt

Zubereitung:

Aus den Zutaten einen feuchten Hefeteig bereiten und gehen lassen. Fett zum Ausbacken in einem hohen Topf erhitzen. Mit 2 Eßlöffeln Teigstückchen hineingeben und goldbraun backen (Fett nicht zu heiß werden lassen, sonst werden die Krebbelchen außen zu dunkel und innen nicht gar).
Noch heiß in Zucker wälzen.

Doughnuts (Krebbelcher)

Ingredients

Metric		Imperial	
1 kg	flour	2 lbs	flour
1 cake	compressed yeast	1 cake	compressed yeast
125 g	sugar	5 oz	sugar
250 ml	milk	1/2 pint	milk
150 g	butter or margarine	6 oz	butter or margarine
6-8	eggs	6-8	eggs
1 t	vanilla extract	1 t	vanilla extract
	pinch of salt		pinch of salt

Method

Sift flour into bowl. Dissolve yeast and 1 teaspoon of sugar in a little lukewarm milk. Let stand for 5 - 10 min. Add yeast mixture to flour and blend in all remaining ingredients. Beat vigorously, blending to a smooth dough. Leave to rise until double its bulk.

Drop from two tablespoons into deep hot fat (not too hot) and fry till golden brown. Drain on kitchen paper. Sprinkle with cinnamon sugar while still hot.

Räiwekechelcher

Zutaten:
- 2 Pfd. Kartoffeln
- 2 Eier
- 1 Zwiebel
- Salz
- 30 g Mehl
- 3 - 4 EBl. Haferflocken
- Backfett

Zubereitung:
Kartoffeln schälen und reiben, übrige Zutaten untermischen und in heißem Fett kleine Kuchen backen.

"Raw" Potato Pancakes (Räiwekechelcher)

Ingredients

Metric		Imperial	
1 kg	potatoes	2 lbs	potatoes
2	eggs	2	eggs
1	onion	1	onion
1/2 t	salt	1/2 t	salt
30 g	flour	3 T	flour
3-4 T	rolled oats	3-4 T	rolled oats

Method

Peel and grate potatoes and onion. Add salt, beaten eggs and dry ingredients. Blend well. Fry on medium hot griddle until brown and turn. Drain on kitchen paper. Serve with spiced apple sauce - using lemon juice, cinnamon and sugar to taste.

Weiße Kechelcher

Zutaten: 500 g Mehl
6 Eier
4 EBl. Zucker
1/4 l Milch

Zubereitung:
Aus den Zutaten einen Rührteig bereiten und - evtl. mit Obst belegt - in Fett in einer Bratpfanne backen.

Pancakes (Weisse Kechelcher)

Ingredients

Metric		Imperial	
500 g	flour	1 lb	flour
6	eggs	6	eggs
4 T	sugar	4 T	sugar
250 ml	milk	1/2 pint	milk

Method

Mix all ingredients and beat until smooth. Fry on hot griddle. Each pancake can be garnished with fruit of your choice while frying.

Geriewene Waffeln

Zutaten:
- 2 Pfd. Mehl
- 1 P. Hefe
- 4 Eier
- 200 g Margarine
- 1 1/2 Teel. Salz
- 2 Pfd. rohe geriebene Kartoffeln
- Milch nach Bedarf

Zubereitung:
Aus den Zutaten einen flüssigen Waffelteig bereiten und löffelweise im gut gefetteten Waffeleisen abbacken.

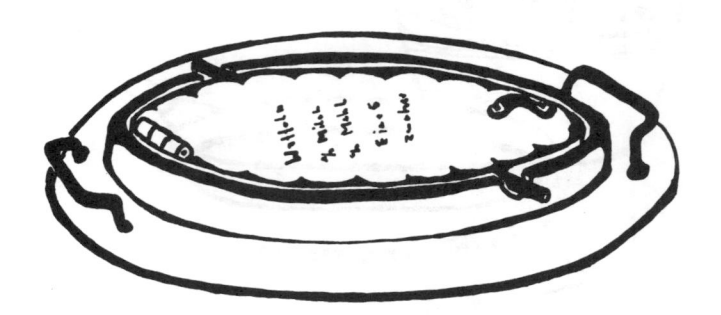

"Raw" Potato Waffles (Geriewene Waffeln)

Ingredients

Metric		Imperial	
1 kg	flour	2 lbs	flour
1 cake	compressed yeast	1 cake	compressed yeast
4	eggs	4	eggs
200 g	margarine	8 oz	margarine
1 1/2 t	salt	1 1/2 t	salt
1 kg	raw grated potatoes	2 lbs	raw grated potatoes
	milk as needed		milk as needed

Method

Blend all ingredients to a moist batter. Bake on hot, well greased waffle iron.

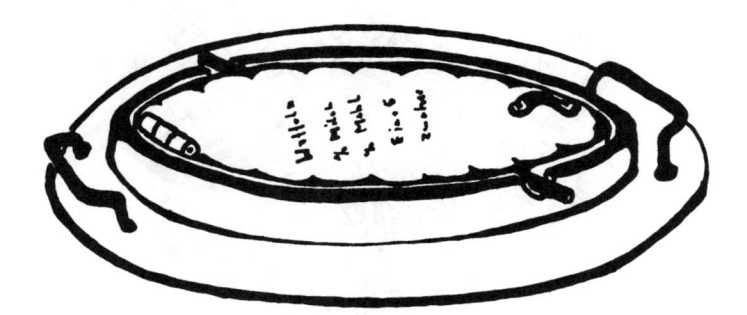

Waffeln beat gekochde Doffeln

Zutaten: 400 g gekochte Kartoffeln
2 Pfd. Mehl
1 P. Hefe
1 - 1¼ ℓ Milch
5 - 10 Eier
125 g Margarine (aufgelöst)

Zubereitung:
Aus Mehl, Hefe, Milch, Eiern und flüssiger Butter Teig herstellen. Kartoffelstücke durch die Quetsche drücken (fein) und unter den Teig rühren.

Cooked Potato Waffles
(Waffeln beat gekochde Doffeln)

Ingredients

Metric		Imperial	
400 g	cooked potatoes	16 oz	cooked potatoes
1 kg	flour	2 lbs	flour
1 packet	dried yeast	1 packet	dried yeast
1-1 1/4 l	milk	2-2 1/2	pints milk
5-10	eggs	5-10	eggs
125 g	melted margarine or butter	5 oz	melted margarine or butter

Method
Mix flour, yeast, milk, eggs and melted margarine to a moist batter. Mash potatoes and blend into batter. Bake in pre-heated waffle iron.

Rohe Doffelskliase

Zutaten: Kartoffeln - je nach Menge
2/3 geriebene Kartoffeln
1/3 gekochte Kartoffeln
etwas Salz
1 Ei (nach Belieben)
Speck
Zwiebeln

Zubereitung:

Die geschälten Kartoffeln werden gerieben und in einem Tuch fest ausgedrückt. Die restlichen Kartoffeln werden am Tag vorher gekocht und zu einem Brei verarbeitet. Dieser wird mit den rohen Kartoffeln vermischt und mit etwas Salz abgeschmeckt. Dann werden aus der Kartoffelmasse kleine Klöße geformt und in Salzwasser gekocht. Wenn die Klöße im Salzwasser oben schwimmen, sind sie gar. Dauer: ca. 15 Min. Anschließend werden die Klöße auf ein Sieb zum Abtropfen gegeben. Dann werden sie mit reichlich Speck und Zwiebeln in der Pfanne knusprig gebraten.

Aus der Kochbrühe wurde früher eine Suppe gekocht: Auf 2 ℓ Kochbrühe 2 EBl. Graupen, Salz (nach Geschmack), Suppengrün

Dumplings made of raw potatoes
(Rohe Doffelskliase)

Ingredients

Depending upon desired mass
2/3 grated raw potatoes
1/3 cooked pototoes
salt to taste
1 egg (optional)
streaks of bacon
onions

Method
Press grated potatoes in kitchen/tea-towel to remove potato fluids. The rest of the potatoes should have been cooked the previous day and then mashed.
Mix raw and cooked potatoes well with each other, adding salt to taste. Blend in egg (optional).
Form small dumplings and let simmer in lightly salted water for about 15 minutes. When dumplings surface, they are done. Drain off excess water. Fry streaks of bacon and sliced onion to a golden brown. Add dumplings until crispy.
The cooking dumpling water can be used as a basis for soups.

Kliase us gekochde Doffeln

Zutaten: 500 g   Kartoffeln (am Vortag kochen)
1   Ei
1 Teel. Salz
65 g   Mehl
etwas   Paniermehl

Zubereitung:
Kartoffeln durch die Presse drücken, mit Ei, Salz und Mehl zu einem Teig verarbeiten und mit feuchten Händen Klöße formen. In kochendes Salzwasser geben und bei offenem Topf garziehen lassen. (Nur kurze Zeit ziehen lassen, daß sie nicht zerfallen.)

Dumplings made from cooked potatoes
(Kliase us gekochde Doffeln)

Ingredients

Metric		Imperial	
500g	potatoes (cooked the previous day)	1 lb	potatoes (cooked the previous day)
1	egg	1	egg
1 t	salt	1 t	salt
65 g	flour	2 1/2 oz	flour
	bread crumbs		bread crumbs

Method
Mash potatoes, blend in egg, salt and flour. Mix in just enough bread crumbs to make a firm dough. Form dumplings with wet hands. Simmer dumplings in lightly salted water until they surface. Do not simmer for too long, dumplings may fall apart.

Breedoffeln

Zutaten: 125 g fetten Speck
2-3 Eßl. Mehl
1 ℓ Wasser
Suppengrün
2 Pfd. Kartoffeln
Mettwürstchen

Zubereitung:

Fetten Speck würfeln und auslassen, Mehl bräunen und mit Wasser ablöschen. Gewürfelte Kartoffeln, kleingeschnittenes Suppengrün und Mettwürstchen hineingeben und garkochen. Mit Salz und Pfeffer abschmecken.

Potato soup (Breedoffeln)

Ingredients

Metric		Imperial	
125 g	bacon	5 oz	bacon
2-3 T	flour	2-3 T	flour
1 l	water	2 pints	water
	soup greens		soup greens
1 kg	potatoes	2 lbs	potatoes
	Bologna sausage		Bologna sausage

Method

Fry diced bacon to a crisp. Sprinkle with flour and fry till golden brown. Add water and stir in rapidly. Add diced potatoes, soup greens and Bologna sausages and simmer till all ingredients are done. Add salt and pepper to taste.

Schdotzköche

Zutaten: 1 kg Kartoffeln
100 g Speck
2-3 Zwiebeln

Zubereitung:
Salzkartoffeln kochen, Wasser abschütten und stampfen. Speck in einer Pfanne auslassen, Zwiebelringe hinzugeben und die gestampften Kartoffeln darauf glattstreichen. Bei kleiner Flamme ca. 10 Min. braten, auf eine Platte stürzen und servieren.

Hierzu reicht man grünen Salat. Im Winter kann man statt Salat auch Zuckerzwetschen dazu essen. Dickmilch schmeckt auch gut dazu.

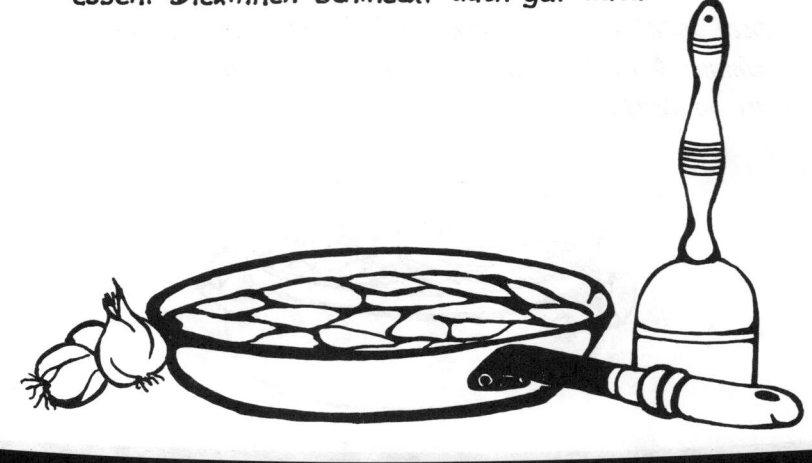

Potato Pancake (Schdotzkoche)

Ingredients

Metric		Imperial	
1 kg	potatoes	2 lbs	potatoes
100 g	bacon	4 oz	bacon
2-3	onions	2-3	onions

Method

Peel, cook and mash potatoes. Fry diced bacon to a crisp, add onion rings. Braise for a while. Spread mashed potatoes over bacon and onions. Fry for about 10 minutes at medium heat. Turn out onto platter and serve hot with a lettuce salad. In Winter, the dish can be served with stewed prunes or curdled milk.

Gequallte Gestallte

Zutaten:
- 2 Pfd. Pellkartoffeln
- 60 g mageren Speck
- 1 große Zwiebel
- 20 g Fett
- 30-40 g Mehl
- 1/4 l Wasser
- Salz, Pfeffer, etwas Essig
- 1 Teel. Senf (nach Geschmack)

Zubereitung:

Speck und Zwiebel in Würfel schneiden, in Fett anbräunen, Mehl dazugeben, anschwitzen, mit Wasser ablöschen, zu einer cremigen Soße verrühren und mit Gewürzen abschmecken. Kartoffeln in dünne Scheiben schneiden und in die Soße geben. Alles zusammen gut erhitzen.

Hierzu wird dicke Milch oder gebratene Blutwurst gereicht.

Sliced Potatoes in Cream Sauce (Gequallte Gestallte)

Ingredients

Metric		Imperial	
1 kg	steamed potatoes	2 lbs	steamed potatoes
60 g	bacon	2 oz	bacon
1	large onion	1	large onion
20 g	lard	1 oz	lard
30-40 g	flour	3-4 T	flour
250 ml	water	1/2 pint	water
salt, pepper, a little vinegar		salt, pepper, a little vinegar	
1 t	mustard (optional)	1 t	mustard (optional)

Method

Braise diced bacon and onions in lard. Sprinkle flour evenly over bacon and onions and allow to brown. Add water and stir to a creamy sauce. Season to taste. Slice potatoes and add to sauce. Serve hot with curdled milk or black pudding.

Zwiwwelsschdibb

Zutaten:
- 100 g Speck
- 1 große Zwiebel
- 4 EBl. Mehl
- 1/2 l Wasser
- Salz
- Pfeffer
- Essig

Zubereitung:

Speck würfeln und auslassen, Zwiebel und Mehl anbräunen, mit kaltem Wasser ablöschen und glattrühren. Mit Salz, Pfeffer und etwas Essig abschmecken.

Hierzu reicht man Pellkartoffeln.

Onion Dip (Zwiwwelsschdibb)

Ingredients:

Metric		Imperial	
100 g	bacon	3 1/2 oz	bacon
1	large onion	1	large onion
4 T	flour	4 T	flour
500 ml	water	1 pint	water
salt, pepper, vinegar		salt, pepper, vinegar	

Method:

Braise diced bacon and onions. Sprinkle in flour and brown. Add cold water and stir to a creamy sauce. Season to taste.
Serve with steamed potatoes.

Sijjerlänner Eierkäs

Zutaten: 6 Eier
1/2 l Milch
1 Teel. Salz
2 EBl. Zucker

Zubereitung:
Alles in ein 1-l-Weckglas füllen und verquirlen.
40 Min. im Wasserbad auf Stufe 2 stocken lassen, in die Eierkäsform füllen und erkalten lassen. Dann stürzen und mit Zucker und Zimt bestreuen.
Eierkäs wird auf Weißbrot gegessen.

Egg Curd (Sijjerlänner Eierkäs)

Ingredients:

Metric		Imperial	
6	eggs	6	eggs
500 ml	milk	1 pint	milk
1 t	salt	1 t	salt
2 T	sugar	2 T	sugar

Method:

Whisk all ingredients and cook in double boiler until mixture thickens. Pour into mould and chill until firm. Turn out onto serving platter and sprinkle with cinnamon sugar. Serve with white bread.

Kiernmelchsobbe

Zutaten:
- 1/2 l Buttermilch
- 1/2 l Milch
- 3 Eßl. Vanille-Puddingpulver
- 2 Eßl. Zucker
- 1 Prise Salz
- Trockenobst

Zubereitung:

Das Puddingpulver mit der Buttermilch anrühren, die Milch inzwischen mit Zucker zum Kochen bringen, die Buttermilchmischung hinzugeben, alles aufkochen lassen und mit Salz abschmecken.
Man kann die Suppe mit weichgekochtem Trockenobst verbessern.

Als Trockenobst nahm man früher

Hotzeln	= getrocknete Birnen
Schnetzeln	= getrocknete Äpfel
gedräjde Gwätsche	= Trockenpflaumen

Buttermilk soup (Kiernmelchsobbe)

Ingredients:

Metric		Imperial	
500 ml	buttermilk	1 pint	buttermilk
500 ml	milk	1 pint	milk
3 T	corn starch	3 T	corn starch
vanilla to taste		vanilla to taste	
2 T	sugar	2 T	sugar
1 pinch	salt	1 pinch	salt
dried fruit		dried fruit	

Method:

Blend corn starch and vanilla into buttermilk. Bring milk an sugar to boil. Whisk in buttermilk mixture. Bring mixture to boil. Add salt to taste. Serve with stewed fruits.

Biersobbe

Zutaten:
- 1 ℓ Milch
- 30 g Butter
- 1 Stange Zimt
- 3 EBl. Mehl
- 1/2 ℓ Bier (Pils)
- 3 EBl. Zucker
- 1 Teel. Salz
- 1 Ei

Zubereitung:

Milch mit Butter und Zimt aufkochen, das angerührte Mehl hinzugeben und durchkochen lassen. Bier hineingeben und bis kurz vors Kochen bringen, mit Salz und Zucker abschmecken und mit dem Eigelb abrühren. Das Eiweiß zu Schnee schlagen und leicht unterheben.

Beer soup (Biersobbe)

Ingredients:

Metric		Imperial	
1 l	milk	2 pints	milk
30 g	butter	1 oz	butter
1 stick of	cinnamon	1 stick of	cinnamon
3 T	flour	3 T	flour
500 ml	beer	1 pint	beer
3 T	sugar	3 T	sugar
1 t	salt	1 t	salt
1	egg	1	egg

Method:

Bring milk, butter and cinnamon to the boil. Mix flour and a little milk to a paste. Whisk into hot milk and allow to boil once more. Add beer and heat to boiling point. Add salt and sugar to taste and whisk in egg yolk. Carefully blend in stiffly beaten egg white.

Gwätschekrud

__Zutaten:__   10 Pfd. ausgekernte Zwetschen
  3 Pfd. Zucker

__Zubereitung:__
Die Zwetschen in einen Topf geben, Zucker darüber streuen, 12 Std. stehen lassen. Auf Stufe 1 2 Std. zugedeckt, dann 3 Std. aufgedeckt kochen (nicht rühren!). Danach 1/2 Std. auf Stufe 2 stark kochen und ständig rühren, bis es steif wird.
1 Likörglas Zwetschenwasser oder Rum unterrühren.

Plum Jam (Gwätschekrud)

Ingredients:

Metric		Imperial	
5 kg	stoned plums	10 lb	stoned plums
1.5 kg	sugar	3 lb	sugar

Method:

Put plums into large saucepan. Sprinkle with sugar and let stand for approximately 12 hours. Place lid on saucepan and cook for 2 hours at low heat. Remove lid and allow to cook for a further 3 hours. Do not stir. Cook plum mixture for another half an hour over moderate fire to a stiff jam while constantly stirring. Finally, stir in one liqueur glass of plum schnapps or rum.

Ruetwänggwätsche

Zutaten:
- 10 Pfd. Pflaumen
- 2-3 Pfd. Zucker
- 2 l Rotwein
- 3-5 Nelken
- 1 Stange Zimt
- 1 P. Einmachhilfe

Zubereitung:

Alle Zutaten aufkochen und Einmachhilfe unterrühren (es darf dann nicht mehr kochen).

Plums in red wine (Ruetwänggwätsche)

Ingredients:

Metric		Imperial	
5 kg	plums	10 lb	plums
1-1.5 kg	sugar	2-3 lb	sugar
2 l	red wine	4 pints	red wine
3-5	cloves	3-5	cloves
1 stick of cinnamon		1 stick of cinammon	

Method:
Bring all ingredients to the boil. Fill preserving jars. Seal.

You cannot get out of a saucepan what you have not put into it.
Czech proverb

Was man in den Topf nicht hineintut, kommt auch nicht heraus.
Tschechisches Sprichwort

Soups, Stews and Casseroles

(Suppen und Eintöpfe)

Siegerländer Hirtentopf

Zutaten:
- 300 g Rindergulasch
- 300 g Schweinegulasch
- 250 g Zwiebeln
- 1-2 Knoblauchzehen (nach Belieben)
- 500 g Paprikaschoten
- 500 g Tomaten
- 500 g Kartoffeln
- 1 kl. Dose Brechbohnen
- 4 EBl. Öl
- 1 l Würfel- oder gekörnte Brühe
- Salz, Pfeffer, Paprika, gemahlener Kümmel
- 1/8 l saure Sahne

Zubereitung:

Fleischwürfel waschen, abtropfen lassen und trockentupfen. Geschälte Zwiebeln grob hacken. Knoblauchzehen schälen und mit etwas Salz zerdrücken. Paprikaschoten halbieren, vierteln, Stiele, Adern, Kerne entfernen, waschen, abtropfen lassen und in Streifen schneiden. Tomaten kurz in siedendes Wasser legen, enthäuten. Stengelansätze wegschneiden und das Tomatenfleisch zerkleinern. Kartoffeln schälen, waschen, abtropfen lassen und in Würfel schneiden. Brechbohnen abtropfen lassen.

Siegerlaender Shepherds Stew
(Siegerländer Hirtentopf)

Ingredients:

Metric		Imperial	
300 g	cubed beef	12 oz	cubed beef
300 g	cubed pork	12 oz	cubed pork
250 g	onions	10 oz	onions
1-2	cloves of garlic (optional)	1-2	cloves of garlic (opt.)
500 g	sweet peppers (red and green)	1 lb	sweet peppers (red and green)
500 g	tomatoes	1 lb	tomatoes
500 g	potatoes	1 lb	potatoes
1 small can broken green beans		1 small can broken green beans	
4 T	oil	4 T	oil
1 l	stock	2 pints	stock
125 ml	soured cream	1/4 pint	soured cream

salt, pepper, paprika, caraway seed

Method:

Wash meat cubes, dry them with kitchen paper. Peel and roughly chop onions. Peel garlic and place on a plate with some salt. Using a round ended knife, rub salt against clove to crush garlic. Cut peppers in half lengthwise, discard seeds, core and white pith. Wash the peppers and cut into strips.

Dann in einem großen Schmortopf Öl erhitzen. Darin Fleischwürfel unter ständigem Rühren rundherum anbraten. Zwiebeln und Knoblauch dazugeben. Mit einem Eßlöffel Paprikapulver bestäuben und leicht rösten. Mit ca. 1/2 l kochendem Wasser aufgießen und mit Salz, Pfeffer und Kümmel würzen. Bei geschlossenem Topf eine Stunde schmoren lassen. Danach Paprikaschotenstreifen, kleingeschnittene Tomaten, Kartoffelwürfel und Brechbohnen hinzufügen. Mit heißer Brühe auffüllen. Gut miteinander vermischen und zugedeckt nochmals 45 Min. garen. Zuletzt den Siegerländer Hirtentopf mit Salz, Pfeffer, Paprika und Kümmel herzhaft abschmecken. Vom Herd nehmen und mit saurer Sahne verfeinern. Sofort in eine vorgewärmte Schüssel füllen und heiß servieren.
Dazu knuspriges Weißbrot oder Bauernschnitten reichen.

Cover tomatoes with boiling water. Leave for 1 minute, then drain, peel and roughly chop. Peel potatoes, wash, drain and cut into
cubes. Drain green beans. Heat oil in a large saucepan. Put the meat-cubes into hot oil and brown on all sides. Add onions and roast lightly. Add 1/2 l boiling water and season to taste with salt, pepper and caraway seed. Cover and let cook for one hour. Then add peppers, tomatoes, potato cubes and green beans. Add hot stock and blend in well. Let simmer for another 45 minutes. Finally, add salt, pepper, paprika and caraway seed to taste. Remove from heat and blend in soured cream.
Put into warm serving dish immediately and serve hot with crispy white bread or brown bread (Backes leaven bread).

Herbsteintopf

Zutaten: 375 g Schweineschulter u. Rinderbug gemischt
3 Zwiebeln
2 Knoblauchzehen
1 EBl. Butter oder Margarine
1 Teel. Thymian
Salz, gemahlener schwarzer Pfeffer
3 Stangen Lauch
3 Karotten
1 Sellerieknolle
1 Wirsingkopf
3 mittelgroße mehlige Kartoffeln
1 Lorbeerblatt

Zubereitung:

Fleisch in 2 cm große Würfel schneiden. Zwiebeln und Knoblauch hacken und in Fett gelb dünsten. Fleisch, Thymian, Salz, Pfeffer und 1/2 l Wasser zugeben und zugedeckt bei schwacher Hitze 30 Min. kochen. Gemüse putzen, in 2 cm breite Streifen oder Würfel schneiden. Schichtweise in Topf geben, leicht salzen und pfeffern. Fleisch mit Brühe daraufgießen. Lorbeerblatt zufügen und das Ganze bei geschlossenem Topf weitere 30 Min. kochen.
Mit Bauernbrot servieren - dazu ein kühles Helles.

Autumn casserole (Herbsteintopf)

Ingredients:

Metric		Imperial	
375 g	meat (partly pork, partly beef)	15 oz	meat (partly pork, partly beef)
3	onions	3	onions
2	cloves of garlic	2	cloves of garlic
1 T	butter or margarine	1 T	butter or margarine
1 t	thyme	1 t	thyme
	salt, black pepper		salt, black pepper
3	medium-sized leeks	3	medium-size leeks
3	carrots	3	carrots
1	heart of celery	1	heart of celery
1	savoy	1	savoy
3	medium-sized potatoes	3	medium-sized potatoes
1	bay leaf	1	bay leaf

Method

Cut meat into medium-sized pieces. Peel and roughly chop onions. Peel cloves of garlic and place on a saucer with salt. Using a round-ended knife, rub salt against cloves to crush garlic. Heat some margarine or butter in a saucepan. Braise onions and garlic until golden brown. Add meat, thyme, salt, pepper and 0,5 l (1 pint) of water. Cover and leave to cook over a moderate heat for 30 minutes. Clean the vegetables and cut either into strips or cubes. Alternately arrange vegetables layer by layer in a large casserole. Season with salt and pepper. Spread meat mixture over vegetables. Add stock and bay-leaf. Cover casserole and let simmer for another 30 minutes. Serve with brown bread and beer.

Fleischwurst-Allerlei

Zutaten:
- 2 dicke Zwiebeln
- 2 grüne Paprikaschoten
- 20 g Margarine oder 2 EBl. Öl
- 1/8 l heiße Fleischbrühe (Würfel)
- 350 g Fleischwurst
- 1 EBl. Paprika edelsüß
- je 1 Prise gem. Kümmel und Majoran
- weißer Pfeffer, Salz
- 2 EBl. Tomatenketchup

Zubereitung:

Zwiebeln in große Scheiben schneiden. Paprikaschoten halbieren, entkernen, waschen und in Streifen schneiden. Margarine oder Öl in einer Pfanne erhitzen. Zwiebelscheiben darin hellgelb werden lassen. Paprikastreifen dazugeben. Unter Rühren 5 Min. anbraten, dann die heiße Fleischbrühe zugießen. 15 Min. dünsten lassen. Fleischwurst häuten, in grobe Würfel schneiden und dazugeben. Mit Paprika edelsüß, Kümmel, Majoran, weißem Pfeffer, wenig Salz und Tomatenketchup würzen.
Kräftig abschmecken und servieren.
Beilagen: Kartoffelpüree oder Bauernbrot
Als Getränk paßt Bier ausgezeichnet dazu.

Pork sausage hotchpotch (Fleischwurst-Allerlei)

Ingredients:

Metric		Imperial	
2	large onions	2	large onions
2	sweet green peppers	2	sweet green peppers
20 g	margarine or 2 T cooking oil	1 oz	
125 ml	hot stock (cubes)	1/4 pint	hot stock
350 g	pork sausage	14 oz	pork sausage
1 T	mild paprika	1 T	mild paprika
1 pinch each of caraway, majoram white pepper and salt		1 pinch each of caraway, marjoram white pepper and salt	
2 T	ketchup	2 T	ketchup

Method

Slice onions. Cut peppers in half lengthwise, discard seeds, core and white pith. Wash the peppers amd cut into strips. Heat margarine or oil in cooking pan. Fry sliced onions till golden brown. Add peppers. Fry whilst continually stirring for about 5 min. Pour in hot stock and allow to simmer for about 15 min. Remove skin from sausages. Dice sausage meat and stir into onion mixture. Season with paprika, caraway, marjoram, pepper. Add some salt to taste. Stir in ketchup.
Serve with mashed potatoes or rye bread.
Beverage: a good beer.

Reistopf

__Zutaten:__   4 Mettwürstchen
2 Zwiebeln
etwas Butter oder Margarine
1 kl. Schüssel geschn. Porree
3/4 - 1 ℓ Brühe
250 g Reis

__Zubereitung:__
Mettwürstchen und Zwiebeln kleinschneiden und im Topf andünsten, kleingeschnittenen Porree dazugeben und mit Brühe auffüllen, zum Kochen bringen, Reis zugeben und umrühren. Im Schnellkochtopf 10 Min. garen.

Rice dish (Reistopf)

Ingredients:

Metric		Imperial	
4	Bologna sausages	4	Bologna sausages
2	onions	2	onions
a bit of butter or margarine		a bit of butter or margarine	
125 g	sliced leek	5 oz	sliced leek
750 ml	stock	1 1/2 pts	stock
250 g	rice	1/2 lb	rice

Method

Slice Bologna sausages and onions. Braise in a pan, add sliced leek, fill up with stock and bring to the boil. Add rice and leave to simmer until rice is tender. Stir occasionally. If you're using a pressure cooker, cook for about 10 min.

Gaisburger Marsch

Zutaten: 500 g Rinderbrust
500 g Suppenknochen
125 g Sellerie
1 kl. Petersilienwurzel
1-2 Stangen Lauch
1/2 Zwiebel
1 Lorbeerblatt
3 Nelken, Pfefferkörner, Salz
500 g Kartoffeln
30 g Butter
3 Zwiebeln
150 g - 200 g Spätzle (vorkochen)

Zubereitung:

Suppenfleisch und Knochen mit kaltem Wasser aufsetzen, aufkochen und abschäumen. Gemüse putzen und mit den Gewürzen zur Brühe geben, alles ca. 1 1/2 Std. kochen. Kartoffeln schälen, waschen und in kleine Würfel schneiden, gesondert in Salzwasser kochen, Fleisch aus der Brühe nehmen und in Würfel schneiden. Brühe sieben.
Butter erhitzen, Zwiebeln in Ringe schneiden und goldgelb braten. Zum Anrichten Fleisch, Kartoffeln und gekochte Spätzle zusammen in eine Suppenterrine schichten und mit der Brühe übergießen. Mit den goldgelben Zwiebeln servieren.

Gaisburger Marsch

Ingredients:

Metric		Imperial	
500 g	brisket of beef	1 lb	brisket of beef
500 g	soup (stewing) bones	1 lb	soup (stewing) bones
125 g	celery	5 oz	celery
1 small	root of parsley	1 small	root of parsley
1-2	leeks	1-2	leeks
1/2	onion	1/2	onion
1	bay leaf	1	bay leaf
3	cloves,	3	cloves
peppercorns, salt		peppercorns, salt	
500 g	potatoes	1/2 lb	potatoes
30 g	butter	1-2 oz	butter
3	onions	3	onions
150g-200g	cooked egg-noodles	6-8 oz	cooked egg-noodles

Method

Place meat and bones in a saucepan and cover with water. Bring to the boil. Remove froth. Clean vegetables and add to stock. Stir in herbs and spices. Cook for 90 min. Peel potatoes, wash and cut into small cubes. Cook potatoes seperately in salted water. Drain when tender. Remove meat and bones from stock. Dice meat. Strain stock. Melt butter in a pan, add sliced onions and braise until golden brown. Alternately put meat, potatoes and boiled noodles in a soup tureen layer by layer. Cover with hot stock. Sprinkle with braised onions before serving.

Rosenkohltopf

Zutaten: 500 g Rosenkohl
1 Eßl. Butter oder Margarine
1 Zwiebel
125 g Reis
1/2 l Wasser oder Fleischbrühe
1 Teel. Salz
150 g Schmierwurst

Zubereitung:

Den Rosenkohl putzen, die Röschen unten kreuzweise einschneiden, damit sie gleichmäßig gar werden. Das Fett heiß werden lassen, die feingehackte Zwiebel und den Reis kurz darin anrösten, Wasser oder Fleischbrühe und Salz hinzufügen. Den Rosenkohl dazugeben, ebenso die Schmierwurst, die mit einem Teelöffel zuvor in kleine Flöckchen zerpflückt wurde.

Das Gericht zugedeckt in 20 Min. bei schwacher Hitze gar werden lassen.

Eignet sich sehr gut zum Einfrieren.

Brussel Sprouts casserole (Rosenkohltopf)

Ingredients:

Metric		Imperial	
500 g	brussel sprouts	1 lb	brussel sprouts
1 T	butter or margarine	1 T	butter or margarine
1	onion	1	onion
125 g	rice	5 oz	rice
500 ml	water or stock	1 pint	water or stock
1 t	salt	1 t	salt
150 g	sausage spread (filling)	6 oz	sausage spread (filling)

Method

Clean and wash brussel sprouts. Cut across base. Heat fat, add finely chopped onions and rice and braise shortly. Add water or stock and salt. Stir in brussel sprouts. Flake sausage filling. Add to casserole. Cover and leave to simmer over moderate heat for about 20 minutes.

Remark: This dish suits very well for freezing.

Paprikaeintopf

Zutaten: 500 g Gehacktes
20 - 30 g Margarine
500 g Tomaten
1 Salatgurke
weißer Pfeffer, Salz, Cayennepfeffer
4 Paprikaschoten
1 Beutel Reis
evtl. Champignons
Paprikapulver

Zubereitung:

Reis kochen, Gehacktes anbraten. Die Tomaten häuten und achteln. Die Salatgurke schälen und kleinschneiden. Tomaten und Gurke zum Hackfleisch geben, mit Pfeffer, Salz und Cayennepfeffer würzen. Paprika waschen, halbieren und in Streifen schneiden und dazugeben. Alles weich dünsten, dann den gekochten Reis und evtl. die Pilze hinzufügen. Nochmals alles kurz aufkochen und mit Paprikapulver abschmecken.

Sweet pepper casserole (Paprikaeintopf)

Ingredients:

Metric		Imperial	
500 g	minced meat	1 lb	minced meat
20-30 g	margarine	1 oz	margarine
500 g	tomatoes	1 lb	tomatoes
1	cucumber	1	cucumber
	white pepper,		white pepper
	salt, cayennepepper		salt, cayennepepper
4	sweet peppers	4	sweet peppers
	(green or red)		(green or red)
250 g	rice	10 oz	rice
	mushrooms (optional)		mushrooms (optional)
	paprikapowder		paprikapowder

Method

Boil rice. Braise minced meat in a large casserole. Cover tomatoes with boiling water for one minute. Drain, peel and cut into eights. Peel and slice cucumber. Add tomatoes and cucmber to the casserole. Season to taste with pepper, salt and cayennepepper. Cut peppers in half lengthwise, discard seeds, core and white pith. Wash and cut into strips. Add to the other ingredients.

Simmer until tender. Then add boiled rice and mushrooms (optional). Bring to the boil and season with paprikapowder. Dish up hot.

Kohlrabitopf (badisch)

Zutaten:
- 8 - 10 Kohlrabi (mit Kraut)
- 2 Zwiebeln
- 40 g Butter oder Margarine
- 2 EBl. Mehl
- 1/2 l Weißwein
- 1/2 l Fleischbrühe
- Salz, Pfeffer, Muskat
- 4 Brühwürste
- 4 Bratwürste

Zubereitung:

Kohlrabi schälen und in Stifte schneiden. Zwiebeln feinschneiden, Butter erhitzen und beides darin 15 Min. dämpfen. Zum Binden Mehl einrühren, mit Wein und Brühe auffüllen und mit Gewürzen abschmecken. Brüh- und Bratwürste kleinschneiden und dazugeben. Kohlrabikraut kleinschneiden und hinzufügen, aufkochen.

Kohlrabi casserole (Kohlrabitopf)

Ingredients:

Metric		Imperial	
8 - 10	kohlrabi (with headleaves)	8-10	kohlrabi (with headleaves)
2	onions	2	onions
40 g	butter or margarine	1 1/2 oz	butter or margarine
2 T	flour	2 T	flour
1 l	white wine	2 pints	white wine
500 ml	stock	1 pint	stock
salt, pepper, grated nutmeg		salt, pepper, grated nutmeg	
4	boiled sausages	4	boiled sausages
4	fried sausages	4	fried sausages

Method:

Peel kohlrabi and cut into strips. Peel and finely chop onions. Melt butter (margarine) and braise kohlrabi and onions for 15 minutes. Sprinkle with the flour. Blend in. Add wine and stock while stirring.

Season to taste with salt, pepper and nutmeg. Slice the sausages and add. Chop the kohlrabi leaves and add. Bring to the boil. Serve hot.

Garniertes Hähnchen (Eintopf)

Zutaten: 1 großes Brathähnchen (1 kg)
Salz, Pfeffer
40 g Palmin
2 Zwiebeln
375 g Champignons
1 kg Kartoffeln
1/8 l Weißwein
1 Bund Petersilie

Zubereitung:

Hähnchen vierteln, mit Salz und Pfeffer einreiben und im Fett gut anbräunen. Zwiebeln würfeln, Champignons halbieren oder in Scheiben schneiden, zum Hähnchen geben und 10 Min. garen. Kartoffeln schälen, grob würfeln und dazugeben, mit Salz und Pfeffer würzen, Wein zugießen und alles 20-25 Min. schmoren lassen.
Abschmecken und mit gehackter Petersilie bestreuen.

Garnished chicken - stew
(Garniertes Hähnchen - Eintopf)

Ingredients:

Metric		Imperial	
1 large	chicken (1 kg)	1 large	chicken (2lb)
	salt, pepper		salt, pepper
40 g	palm butter	1 1/2 oz	palm butter
2	onions	2	onions
375g	mushrooms	15 oz	mushrooms
1 kg	potatoes	2 lb	potatoes
125 ml	white wine	1/4 pint	white wine
	parsley		parsley

Method:
Quarter chicken, wash, dry and rub with salt and pepper. Heat fat and roast chicken until brown. Cut mushrooms in half or slice. Add to roasted chicken and let simmer for 10 minutes. Peel potatoes, dice and add. Season to taste with salt and pepper. Add wine and cover. Let cook over a moderate heat for 20-25 minutes. Season to taste and sprinkle with chopped parsley.

Champignonsuppe

Zutaten: 50 g frische Champignons
1/2 EBl. Butter oder Margarine
3/8 l Kalbsbrühe
1 EBl. Kindergrieß
1 Eigelb
2 EBl. süße Sahne
1 Prise Salz
einige Tropfen Zitronensaft

Zubereitung:
Champignons säubern, in feine Scheiben schneiden und in Butter andünsten, Kalbsbrühe auffüllen, Grieß zugeben, alles unter Rühren aufkochen und ca. 10 Min. garen.
Eigelb mit Sahne verquirlen und in die heiße Suppe einrühren, nicht mehr aufkochen.
Mit Salz und Zitronensaft abschmecken.

Mushroomsoup (Champignonsuppe)

Ingredients:

Metric		Imperial	
50 g	fresh mushrooms	2 oz	fresh mushrooms
1/2 T	butter or margarine	1/2 T	butter or margarine
375 ml	veal stock	3/4 pints	veal stock
1T	semolina	1T	semolina
1	egg yolk	1	egg yolk
2 T	single cream	2T	single cream
1	pinch of salt	1	pinch of salt
some drops of lemon juice		some drops of lemon juice	

Method

Clean mushrooms and slice. Braise in butter, add stock. Add semolina and bring to the boil whilst stirring constantly. Cook for 10 minutes until tender. Beat egg yolk with cream. Stir into hot soup. Do not cook any further. Season to taste with salt and lemon juice.

Krautsuppe

Zutaten: 1 - 1½ l Fleischbrühe
40 g Butter oder Margarine
2 EBl. Mehl
300 g Sauerkraut
Pfeffer
⅛ l saure Sahne
300 g gekochtes Rindfleisch (falls vorhanden)

Zubereitung:

Mehl in Butter hell anschwitzen, mit Brühe ablöschen, das rohe Sauerkraut locker einlegen, restliche Brühe aufgießen. 15 Min. bei schwacher Hitze kochen, saure Sahne einrühren. Falls vorhanden, kann feingewürfeltes gekochtes Rindfleisch in die Suppe gegeben werden.

Cabbage soup (Krautsuppe)

Ingredients:

Metric		Imperial	
1-1 1/2 l	stock	2-3 pints	stock
40 g	butter or margarine	1 1/2	butter or margarine
2 T	flour	2 T	flour
300 g	sauerkraut	300 g	sauerkraut
	pepper		pepper
125 ml	soured cream	1/4 pint	soured cream
300 g	cooked beef (optional)	12 oz	cooked beef (optional)

Method

Melt butter in a saucepan. Add flour and stir the mixture over a low heat until it begins to bubble. Add enough stock, whisking constantly, to make a smooth, lightly thickened blend. Put in the raw sauerkraut. Add rest of stock. Simmer over a moderate heat for 15 minutes. Blend in soured cream. Cut cooked meat into cubes and add to the soup.

Herzhafte Sauerkrautsuppe

Zutaten: 1 kg Hackfleisch
Salz, Pfeffer,
Paprikapulver, Knoblauchsalz.
1 große Dose Sauerkraut
8 Gewürzgurken
1 Tube Tomatenmark
2 l klare Brühe

Zubereitung:

Aus Hackfleisch und Gewürzen kleine Fleischbällchen formen und anbraten, Brühe aufkochen, Zwiebeln und Gurken kleinschneiden.

Alle Zutaten in der Brühe 40 Min. langsam kochen.

Spicy Sauerkraut Soup
(Herzhafte Sauerkrautsuppe)

Ingredients:

Metric		Imperial	
1 kg	ground meat	2 lb	ground meat
	salt, pepper		salt, pepper
	paprika, garlic salt		paprika, garlic salt
500 g	sauerkraut	1 lb	sauerkraut
8	gherkins	8	gherkins
200 g	tomato puree	8 oz	tomato puree
2 l	stock	4 pints	stock

Method

Mix ground meat with spices and form little balls. Fry until brown.
Bring stock to the boil. Chop onions and gherkins. Mix all ingredients into the stock. Cook over a moderate heat for 40 minutes.

Brotsuppe mit Leberwurst

Zutaten: 1 l Fleischbrühe
4 Scheiben Bauernbrot
1 EBl. gehackte Kräuter
(Petersilie, Majoran, Kümmel, Pfeffer)
Salz
4 kleine Leberwürste

Zubereitung:

Brühe erhitzen und kräftig abschmecken. Brot in Würfel schneiden und dazugeben. Leberwurst erhitzen und Wurstfüllung in die Suppe geben. Nicht mehr aufkochen. Frische Kräuter dazugeben und sehr heiß servieren.

Bread soup with liver-sausage
(Brotsuppe mit Leberwurst)

Ingredients:

Metric		Imperial	
1 l	stock	2 pints	stock
4	slices brown bread	4	slices brown bread
1 T	chopped herbes (parsley, majoram)	1 T	chopped herbes (parsley, majoram)
	salt, pepper, ground caraway seed		
4	small liver-sausages	4	small liver-sausages

Method
Bring stock to the boil and season well. Cut bread slices into cubes and add to the stock. Heat liver-sausages, remove skin and add filling to the stock. Don't cook. Add fresh herbes and serve hot.

Echte ungarische Gulaschsuppe

Zutaten:
- 12 mittlere Zwiebeln
- 500 g Rindfleisch (klein gewürfelt)
- 1 l Fleischbrühe (Würfel)
- 100 g Butter oder Schweineschmalz
- 1 gestr. Eßl. Rosenpaprika (scharf)
- 1/2 Teel. schwarzer Pfeffer
- 1 Teel. zerstoßener Kümmel
- 1/2 Teel. Majoran
- 1 Teel. Salz
- 2 Kartoffeln
- 2 frische große Paprikaschoten
- 4 Tomaten oder Tomatenmark
- 1/4 Teel. Knoblauchsalz
- 1/2 Tasse Rotwein

Zubereitung:

Zwiebeln und Fleisch in Würfel schneiden. Fleischbrühe zubereiten, Butter zerlassen, Fleisch dazugeben und 15 Min. unter ständigem Rühren anbraten, Zwiebeln mitrösten. Paprikapulver, Pfeffer, Kümmel, Majoran und Salz dazugeben und mit Fleischbrühe auffüllen. 1 Std. zugedeckt bei schwacher Hitze garen.

Real Hungarian Goulashsoup
(Echte ungarische Gulaschsuppe)

Ingredients:

Metric		Imperial	
12	medium-sized onions	12	medium-sized onions
500 g	beef (cut into small cubes)	1lb	beef (cut into small cubes)
1 l	stock (cubes)	2 pints	stock (cubes)
100g	butter or lard	4 oz	butter or lard
1 level T	paprika (hot)	1 level T	paprika (hot)
1/2 t	black pepper	1/2 t	black pepper
1 t	ground caraway seed	1 t	ground caraway seed
1/2 t	majoram	1/2 t	majoram
1t	salt	1t	salt
2	potatoes	2	potatoes
2	large sweet peppers (red or green)	2	large sweet peppers (red or green)
4	tomatoes or tomatopurée	4	tomatoes or tomatopurée
1/2 t	garlic salt	1/2	garlic salt
1/2	cup red wine	1/2	cup red wine

½ l Wasser zum Kochen bringen. Kartoffelwürfel und Paprikastreifen hinzugeben. Tomaten überbrühen und Schale abziehen. Tomatenfleisch hinzugeben. Nach 15 Min. Kochzeit pürieren, Knoblauchsalz hinzugeben, alles zusammen in die Suppe geben und aufkochen lassen, evtl. noch etwas Wasser zugeben. Zuletzt den Rotwein hinzugeben (nicht mehr kochen lassen).

Method:

Cut onions into small cubes. Prepare stock. Melt butter, add meat cubes and braise for 15 minutes while stirring constantly. Add onions and braise. Season to taste with paprikapowder, pepper, carawayseed, majoram and salt. Add stock. Let simmer for 1 hour over a moderate heat.

Bring 1/2 l (1 pint) water to the boil. Peel potatoes and cut into small cubes. Cut sweet peppers in half lengthwise, discard seeds, core and white pith. Slice into strips. Add to boiling water. To remove skin from tomatoes, cover with boiling water for one minute. Drain, peel, chop and add to potatoes and peppers. Let cook for 15 minutes. Then make a purée of the done potato, pepper, tomato mixture. Add garlic salt and purée to the soup. Add some more hot water if necessary. Finally add the red wine. Do not cook anymore.

Holunderbeersuppe

Zutaten:
- 1 l Holunderbeersaft
- 100 g Zucker
- 5 Gewürznelken
- 1 Zimtstange
- Zitronenschale
- 12 halbierte Pflaumen
- 3 Birnen (in Spalten geschnitten)
- Zitronensaft
- Eischnee

Zubereitung:

Saft mit Zucker und Gewürzen aufkochen, Obst hinzugeben und 10 Min. garkochen. Stärke anrühren und einlaufen lassen, aufkochen, mit Zitronensaft abschmecken, Eischnee daraufgeben und heiß servieren.

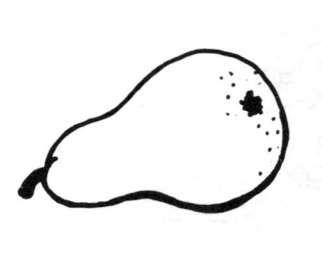

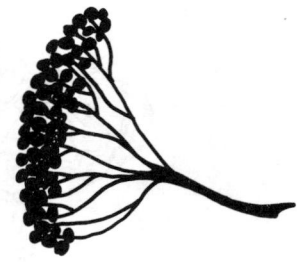

Elder-berry soup (Holunderbeersuppe)

Ingredients:

Metric		Imperial	
1 l	elder-berry juice	2 pints	elder-berry juice
100 g	sugar	4 oz	sugar
5	cloves	5	cloves
1 stick	cinnamon	1 stick	cinnamon
	grated lemon rind		grated lemon rind
12	plums, cut in half	12	plums, cut in half
3	pears, peeled, cored and sliced	3	pears, peeled, cored and sliced
	lemon juice		lemon juice
1 level T	cornflour	1 level T	cornflour
whisked egg white		whisked egg white	

Method:

Mix juice, sugar and spices. Bring to the boil, add fruit and cook for 10 minutes until tender. Blend cornflour with a little water and add to juice and fruit whilst stirring constantly. Cook for one minute. Season to taste with lemon juice. Put whisked egg white on top and serve immediately.

You cannot expect more from an ox than a decent piece of beef.

Proverb

Von einem Ochsen kann man nichts anderes verlangen als ein anständiges Stück Rindfleisch.

Sprichwort

Meat, Poultry and Egg Dishes

(Fleisch, Geflügel und Eier)

Filet - Stroganoff

Zutaten

500g Rinderfilet oder Schweinelenden,
   Salz, Pfeffer, etwas Butter,
1 Zwiebel, 1 saure Gurke,
1 Tomate od. Ketchup, 1 Teel. Senf,
1 kl. Dose Champignons
   etwas Mehl
1 B. süße Sahne, 1 B. saure Sahne,
1 Fondorwürfel, Curry, Salz, Pfeffer.

Zubereitung

Fleisch in Streifen schneiden, in Butter braten, aus dem Topf nehmen, salzen u. pfeffern. Zwiebel, Gurke, Tomate, Senf, u. Champignons in Fett schmoren, süße u. saure Sahne u. Fondor zugeben, mit Curry, Salz u. Pfeffer abschmecken. Zu Toast oder Reis servieren.

Filet - Stroganoff

Ingredients

Metric	Imperial
500 g filet of beef or pork sirloin	1 lb filet of beef or pork sirloin
salt, pepper, butter	salt, pepper, butter
1 onion	1 onion
1 large gherkin	1 large gherkin
1 tomato or some ketchup	1 tomato or some ketchup
1 t mustard	1 t mustard
200 g fresh mushrooms (or 1 small can mushrooms)	8 oz fresh mushrooms (or 1 small can mushrooms)
some flour	some flour
200 ml single cream	1/2 pint single cream
200 ml soured cream	1/2 pint soured cream
1 bouillon cube	1 bouillon cube
curry, salt, pepper	curry, salt, pepper

Method

Slice meat into strips. Fry in butter, remove from frying pan and season with salt and pepper. Braise sliced onions, sprinkle in flour. Add diced gherkin, tomato, mustard and mushrooms in butter. Blend in cream and season with bouillon cube, salt and pepper. Stir in meat and re-heat. Serve on toast or with rice.

Kasseler spezial

Zutaten

1000g Kartoffeln, 1000g Kasseler, 1/8 l Oel, 1000g tiefgefr. Bohnen, Pfeffer, Salz

Zubereitung

Die Kartoffeln grob würfeln u. 6 Min. in Salzwasser vorgaren. In die Mitte einer Pfanne das Fleisch legen u. das Oel dazugießen.

Die Kartoffel auf die eine Seite des Fleisches u. die Bohnen auf die andere Seite des Fleisches legen. Bohnen mit etwas Salz u. Pfeffer würzen. Die obenliegenden Kartoffeln mit etwas Oel einpinseln, damit sie sich nicht verfärben. Im Backofen bei 225° 70 Minuten garen.

Cured Spare-rib of Pork Kasseler Style (Kasseler Spezial)

Ingredients

Metric		Imperial	
1 kg	potatoes	2 lbs	potatoes
1 kg	cured spare-rib	2 lbs	cured spare-rib
125 ml	cooking oil	1/4 pint	cooking oil
1 kg	frozen or fresh broken green beans	2 lbs	frozen or fresh broken green beans
salt and pepper		salt and pepper	

Method

Peel potatoes, dice and cook in lightly salted water for about 5 minutes. Place meat in centre of casserole. Add oil. Arrange seasoned beans on the one and potatoes on the other side of meat. Brush upper layer of potatoes with oil to prevent discoloring. Bake in hot oven for 70 minutes at 225° C (450° F).

Geschnetzeltes

Zutaten

350g	Schweineschnitzel
2	Zwiebel
1	Dose Champignons
1	Glas Tomatenpaprika
1	Löffel Margarine
1/4	Liter Weißwein (nach Geschmack)
1/8	Liter süße Sahne
2	Teel. Instand helle Soße
	Salz, Cayennepfeffer, etwas Zitronensaft

Zubereitung

Schnitzel in feine Streifen schneiden u. im Fett fertig braten. Margarine in einen Topf geben, aufschäumen

Sliced pork in cream sauce (Geschnetzeltes)

Ingredients:

Metric		Imperial	
350 g	pork filet	3/4 lb	pork filet
2 onions		2 onions	
200 g	fresh mushrooms	8 oz	fresh mushrooms
(or its equivalent weight in can)		(or its equivalent weight in can)	
1 regular sized jar of pickled red sweet peppers		1 regular sized jar of pickled red sweet peppers	
1 T	margarine	1 T	margarine
250 ml	white wine	1/2 pint	white wine
125 ml	single cream	1/4 pint	single cream
2 t	instant white sauce	2 t	instant white sauce
salt, cayenne pepper, a little lemon juice		salt, cayenne pepper, a little lemon juice	

Method:

Cut meat into small slices. Braise in fat until done. Braise onions in heated margarine until golden brown. Clean and slice mushrooms. Add mushrooms and pickled red sweet peppers to the onions.

lassen, Zwiebelwürfel dazu hell anbraten. Champignons u. Tomatenpaprika hinzufügen, Weißwein eingießen u. etwas verkochen lassen. Sahne u. Soßenpulver einrühren, Fleisch untermischen u. kurz aufkochen lassen. Zuletzt mit Salz, Pfeffer u. Zitronensaft abschmecken.

<u>Beilage:</u> Reis, Nudeln, Kartoffeln

Add white wine and bring to the boil. Blend in single cream and instant white sauce powder. Add meat and bring to the boil. Remove from heat and season to taste with salt, pepper and lemon juice.
Serve with rice, noodles or potatoes.

Bratwurst-Schnitzel

Zutaten

4 Schweineschnitzel
Bratwurstmett
Champignons
1 Zwiebel, etwas süße Sahne

Zubereitung

Schnitzel auf ein Blech legen, Bratwurstmett ca. ½-1cm dick darauf streichen u. ganze Champignons darauf verteilen. (Pilze evtl. mit Zwiebel andünsten) Nun die süße Sahne darüber geben.
Ca. 1 Std. bei 180° im Backofen überbacken.
Dazu Backkartoffeln mit Kräuterbutter.

Sausage Escalopes (Bratwurstschnitzel)

Ingredients:

Metric   Imperial

4 pork escalopes
raw filling of 3-4 frying sausages
mushrooms
1 onion
single cream

Method

Lay escalopes on a buttered baking tin. Spread sausage filling 1/2 - 1 cm (1/2 inch) thick over the escalopes. Braise whole mushrooms with diced onion. Cover escalopes with mushrooms. Pour over some single cream. Bake in a preheated oven at 180°C (350°F) for about 1 hour.

Serve with baked potatoes and herb butter.

Zwiebelschnitzel

Zutaten
4 Schnitzel, 500g Zwiebeln
250g gek. Schinken,
2 Becher süße Sahne

Zubereitung
Schnitzel braten u. aus der Pfanne nehmen. Zwiebel u. Schinken im Fett dünsten, mit Salz u. Pfeffer würzen. Die Schnitzel in die Fettpfanne (Backofen) legen, die gedünsteten Zwiebeln u. Schinken darübergeben u. mit der süßen Sahne übergießen.
Über Nacht stehen lassen.
Bei 125° ca 1½ Stunden im Backofen backen.

Onion escalopes (Zwiebelschnitzel)

Ingredients:

Metric		Imperial	
4	escalopes (veal or pork)	4	escalopes (veal or pork)
500 g	onions	1 lb	onions
250 g	cooked ham	10 oz	cooked ham
400 ml	single cream	3/4 pint	single cream

Method:

Braise escalopes until done. Remove from pan. Dice onions and ham. Braise until golden. Season to taste with salt and pepper. Put escalopes in a buttered baking tin.

Spread braised onions and ham over the escalopes. Pour single cream over all. Let soak for about 12 hours. Then bake in preheated oven at 125°C (250°F) for 90 min.

Früchtegulasch

Zutaten

1 Kg. Gulasch halb u. halb,
1 Pfd. Zwiebel, 1 Gl. Zigeunersoße,
1 D. Ananas o. Saft, 1 D. Pfirsiche o. Saft,
1 D. Champignons m. etwas Saft,
1 Gl. Sauerkirschen m. Saft,
1 B. süße Sahne, etwas Rotwein od. Cognac

Zubereitung

Gulasch m. Zwiebel in Öl anbraten. Mit Zigeunersoße auffüllen u. garen, ca 1-1½ Std. Früchte u. Pilze zugeben, langsam erwärmen, nicht kochen. Zum Schluß Sahne zugeben u. evtl. mit Cognac od. Rotwein verfeinern.

Mit Weißbrot oder Reis servieren.

Goulash with fruit (Früchtegulasch)

Ingredients:

Metric		Imperial	
500 g	cubed pork	1 lb	cubed pork
500 g	cubed beef	1 lb	cubed beef
500 g	onions	1 lb	onions
1 jar	hot barbecue sauce	1 jar	hot barbecue sauce
1 can	mushrooms	1 can	mushrooms
1 jar	sour cherries and juice	1 jar	sour cherries and juice
200ml	single cream	3/8 pint	single cream
some red wine or cognac		some red wine or cognac	

Method:

Dice onions. Braise cubed meat and onions in hot oil until brown. Add hot barbecue sauce. Let cook for 1-1 1/2 hours until done. Add fruit and mushrooms. Do not boil anymore. When fruit and mushrooms are heated, finally add single cream and season to taste with some cognac or red wine (optional).

Serve with white bread or rice.

Gekochtes Kalbfleisch in Dillsosse

Zutaten

1500g Kalbfleisch, Suppengemüse, 1 Zwiebel, Salz, Pfeffer, Zitrone, frischer Dill, Sahne, Mehl, Butter

Zubereitung

In Würfel geschn. Kalbfleisch mit geschn. Zwiebeln u. Gemüse andünsten. Mit Brühe bis 2cm über dem Fleisch auffüllen u. gardämpfen. Fleisch u. Gemüse in eine feuerfeste Form füllen u. warm stellen. Die Brühe wird mit etwas Mehl gebunden u. mit Sahne, Dill u. Zitrone verfeinert. Geben Sie die Soße über das Fleisch u. servieren Sie Reis dazu.

Cooked Veal in Dill Sauce
(Gekochtes Kalbfleisch in Dillsoße)

Ingredients:

Metric	Imperial
1500 g veal	3 lb veal
soup greens	soup greens
1 onion	1 onion
stock	stock
salt, pepper, lemon juice	salt, pepper, lemon juice
fresh dill	fresh dill
single cream	single cream
flour and butter	flour and butter

Method:
Dice veal. Chop onion and soup greens. Braise and season with salt and pepper. Cover with stock. Simmer until done. Drain meat and vegetables. Fill into serving dish. Keep warm. Thicken stock with flour. Season to taste. Stir in cream, dill and lemon juice. Pour sauce over meat and vegetables.
Serve with rice.

Kalbsherz in Zitronensoße

Zutaten

2 Kalbsherzen, 2 Zwiebel, 2 Nelken,
8 Pfefferkörner, 1 Lorbeerblatt,
1 unbeh. Zitrone, Salz.
1½ l. Wasser, 2 Eßl. Butter, 1 Pr. Zucker,
3 gestr. Eßl. Mehl, 2 Eigelb,
2 Eßl. Kapern.

Zubereitung

Die Kalbsherzen mit den Zwiebeln, (vierteln) allen Gewürzen u. der dünn abgeschälten Zitronenschale ins kochende Wasser geben. Im geschl. Topf ca. 1½ - 1¾ Std. garen. Fleisch herausnehmen u. warmstellen. Brühe durchseihen.
Für die Soße Butter u. Mehl hell anschwitzen, ½ l. Brühe zugeben,

Hearts of veal in lemon sauce
(Kalbsherz in Zitronensauce)

Ingredients:

Metric		Imperial	
2	hearts of veal	2	hearts of veal
2	onions	2	onions
2	cloves	2	cloves
8	peppercorns	8	peppercorns
1	bay-leaf	1	bay-leaf
1	untreated lemon	1	untreated lemon
	salt		salt
1500 ml	water	3 pints	water
2 T	butter	2 T	butter
1 pinch	of sugar	1 pinch	of sugar
3 level T	flour	3 level T	flour
2	egg yolks	2	egg yolks
2 T	capers	2 T	capers

Method:

Peel and quarter onion. Thinly peel lemon. Bring water to the boil. Add veal hearts, onions, spices and lemon peel. Cover and simmer for 90-100 minutes.

aufkochen lassen u. mit Salz, Zitronen=
saft u. Zucker abschmecken. Mit den
2 Eigelb binden, nicht mehr kochen.
Kapern hinzufügen.
Die Kalbsherzen in Scheiben schnei=
den, in eine Schüssel geben u. mit
der Soße übergießen.

Statt der Kalbsherzen kann man
auch Schweineherzen nehmen oder
kleine Pökelzungen.

Remove veal from sauce pan. Keep warm. Sieve stock. Melt butter, sprinkle in flour while stirring continually until golden. Add 500 ml (1 pint) stock while stirring constantly. Bring to the boil. Reduce heat. Season to taste with salt, lemon juice and sugar. Blend in 2 egg yolks until sauce thickens. Do not cook anymore. Add capers. Slice veal hearts. Put in a serving dish and cover with sauce.

Tip: Instead of veal hearts you can use cured tongue.

Schlesisches Himmelreich

Zutaten

500 - 700g Rauchfleisch,
250 g getr. Pflaumen, Äpfel und Birnen,
2 Eßl. Mehl, 3 Eßl. Zucker,
1 Eßl. Zitronensaft, 1 Pr. Salz

Zubereitung

Rauchfleisch aufsetzen u. vorkochen, Obst einweichen u. 3/4 Std. mit dem Fleisch noch kochen. Bei niedriger Hitze garen. Mehl mit Wasser verrühren u. zugeben, mit Zucker, Zitronensaft u. Salz abschmecken. Dazu reicht man Kartoffel- oder Semmelklöße.

Smoked meat with fruit (Schlesisches Himmelreich)

Ingredients:

Metric		Imperial	
500-700 g	smoked meat	1-1 1/2 lb	smoked meat
250 g	dried plums, apples and pears	1/2 lb	dried plums, apples and pears
2 T	flour	2 T	flour
3 T	sugar	3 T	sugar
1 T	lemon juice	1 T	lemon juice
1	pinch of salt	1	pinch of salt

Method:

Pre-cook cured meat. Soak diced fruit for 45 minutes. Cook with smoked meat at low heat. Blend flour with some water and add to meat and fruit. Stir in sugar and lemon juice. Add salt to taste.

Serve with potatoes or bread dumplings (as described in farmer's treat).

Bauernschmaus

Zutaten

250g Sauerkraut, 1 Zwiebel, Mehl, Öl, Kümmel, Salz, Zucker, Pfeffer, 1/16 l. Milch, 4 alte Brötchen, 1 Ei, gehackte Petersilie, 400g Kasseler, 400g Schweinefleisch, 2 Paar Mettwürstchen

Zubereitung

Geschnittene Zwiebeln anrösten, Sauerkraut u. Kümmel hinzugeben, mit etwas Brühe auffüllen u. garen.
Semmelknödel: Brötchen in Scheiben schneiden. Milch, Ei, Salz u. Petersilie verquirlen u. auf die geschn. Brötchen gießen. Ziehen lassen. Zu Knödeln formen u. in siedendem Wasser kochen. Schweine=

Farmer's treat (Bauernschmaus)

Ingredients:

Metric		Imperial	

For sauerkraut:
250 g	sauerkraut	1/2 lb	sauerkraut
1	onion	1	onion
flour, oil, carawayseed		flour, oil, carawayseed	
salt, sugar, pepper		salt, sugar, pepper	

For bread-dumplings:
125 ml	milk	1/4 pint	milk
4	dried rolls	4	dried rolls
1	egg	1	egg
chopped parsley		chopped parsley	

Meat:
400 g	cured spare-rib of pork	16 oz	cured spare-rib of pork
400 g	pork	16 oz	pork
4	Bologna sausages	4	Bologna sausages

Method:

Sauerkraut:
Braise diced onion. Add sauerkraut and carawayseed. Fill up with some stock and simmer until done.

Fleisch braten u. mit Kasseler garen.
Servieren Sie Fleisch, Würstchen, Kraut
u. Knödel in einer Kasserolle.

Bread-dumplings:
Slice rolls. Mix milk, egg, salt and choppped parsley. Beat well and pour over sliced rolls. Let soak. Form dumplings and cook in simmering salted water until done.

Meat:
Braise pork and prepare with spare-rib of pork and Bologna sausages as usual.

Serve meat, sausages, sauerkraut and dumplings in one casserole.

Rouladen aus Hackfleisch

Zutaten

400g Hackfleisch halb u. halb
1 gr, feingeh. Zwiebel
3/4 Tasse Weizenkleie
1 Ei, 1/2 Teel. Salz
Pfeffer, Muskat
1 gr. Gewürzgurke
8 Scheiben mag. Speck
Fett zum Braten
1/4 l. Brühe
2 Eßl. Tomatenketchup
etwas Mehl, Pfeffer,
Salz u. Petersilie

Minced meat rolls
(Rouladen aus Hackfleisch)

Ingredients:

Metric		Imperial	
200 g	minced pork	8 oz	minced pork
200 g	minced beef	8 oz	minced beef
1 large	onion	1 large	onion
175 g	wheaten bran	7 oz	wheaten bran
1	egg	1	egg
1/2 t	salt	1/2 t	salt
	pepper, grated nutmeg		pepper, grated nutmeg
1 large	gherkin	1 large	gherkin
8 slices	lean bacon	8 slices	lean bacon
250 ml	stock	1/2 pint	stock
2 T	ketchup	2 T	ketchup
	some flour, pepper, salt and chopped parsley		some flour, pepper, salt and chopped parsley

Zubereitung

Weizenkleie mit 1/4 Tasse Wasser anfeuchten, mit Hackfleisch, Ei, Zwiebel u. Gewürzen mischen. Gewürzgurke längs in 8 Streifen schneiden. Hackfl. in 8 Port. teilen und die Gurkenstreifen darin einrollen. Mit je 1 Sch. Speck umwickeln u. in eine gef. Form legen. Bei mittl. Hitze 20 Min. im Backofen garen. Brühe aufgießen u. weitere 10. Min. garen. Fleisch herausnehmen, Ketchup in die Soße geben, mit Mehl binden u. mit Salz u. Pfeffer abschmecken. Fleisch in die Soße geben und mit Petersilie garnieren.

Dazu Reis servieren.

Method:

Soak bran in 70 ml (4 T) water. Mix with minced meat, egg, onion and spices. Cut gherkin lengthwise in 8 strips. Divide meat mixture into 8 portions. Roll strip of gherkin into each portion of meat. Fold one streak of bacon around each roll. Put meat rolls in a buttered casserole. Bake in pre-heated oven at a moderate heat (175°C/350°F) for 20 minutes. Add stock and leave to cook in oven for another 10 minutes. Remove meat rolls. Keep warm. Add ketchup to stock and thicken with some flour while stirring constantly. Season to taste with salt and pepper. Return meat to sauce and garnish with chopped parsley.
Serve with rice.

Frikadellen mit Orangen

Zutaten: 125g Rinderhack
125g Schweinehack
2 große Orangen
50g Kokosraspeln
1 Ei
1 Tasse Semmelbrösel
Salz
2 Eßl. Rosinen
50g Margarine

Zubereitung: Hack mit feingewürfeltem Obst u. übrigen Zutaten mischen. 4 Frikadellen formen u. goldbraun braten. Auf Salatblätter anrichten.

Meatballs with Oranges
(Frikadellen mit Orangen)

Ingredients:

Metric		Imperial	
125 g	minced beef	5 oz	minced beef
125 g	minced pork	5 oz	minced pork
2 large	oranges	2 large	oranges
50 g	dessicated coconut	2 oz	dessicated coconut
1	egg	1	egg
2 T	raisins	2 T	raisins
50 g	margarine	2 oz	margarine

Method:
Peel oranges. Cut fruit into small cubes. Evenly mix all ingredients. Add enough bread crumbs to make a stiff but smooth dough. Form 4 meatballs. Fry until done and serve on lettuce leaves.

Orangensoße z. Putenbraten

Zutaten

    Saft von 3 Orangen
1   Eßl. Zucker
2   Teel. gerieb. Meerrettich
    (kann auch aus dem Glas sein)
1   Teel. Essig, 1 gerieb. Apfel

Zubereitung

Alles zusammen erhitzen u. mit etwas Stärkepuder binden.

Zu Putenkeulen oder – Schenkeln servieren.

Orangesauce to serve with roast turkey
(Orangensauce zum Putenbraten)

Ingredients:

juice of	3 oranges
1 T	sugar
2 t	fresh ground horseradish
1 T	vinegar
1	grated apple

Method:
Mix well all ingredients. Heat and thicken with some corn starch while stirring constantly.
Serve with roast turkey.

Hähnchenkeule mit Zitrone

Zutaten

6-8 tiefgefr. Hähnchenkeulen,
4 Zwiebel, 1/8 l. fr. Zitronensaft,
1 Knoblauchzehe, 1 Teel. Salz,
1 Teel. schw. Pfeffer, 1 Eßl. Zucker,
4 Eßl. Weißwein, 4 Eßl. Butter,
etwas süße Sahne

Zubereitung

Hähnchenkeulen auf Zwiebelscheiben in einen Bräter legen. Zitronensaft, gequetschten Knoblauch und übrige Zutaten aufkochen u. über die Keulen löffeln. Nach 30 Minuten im vorgeheizten Ofen bei 200° ca. 30-35 Min. garen, öfter wenden. Bratensoße mit süßer Sahne und Zitrone abschmecken.

Chicken drumstick with lemon (Hähnchenkeule mit Zitrone)

Ingredients:

Metric		Imperial	
6-8	chicken drumsticks	6-8	chicken drumsticks
4	onions	4	onions
125 ml	lemon juice	1/4 pint	lemon juice
1	clove of garlic	1	clove of garlic
1 t	salt	1 t	salt
1 t	black pepper	1 t	black pepper
1 T	sugar	1 T	sugar
4 T	white wine	4 T	white wine
4 T	butter	4 T	butter
	some single cream		some single cream

Method:

Peel and slice onions. Put in a buttered casserole. Arrange chicken drumsticks over onion slices. Peel clove of garlic and place on a saucer with salt. Using a round-ended knife, rub salt against clove to crush garlic. Mix crushed garlic, all spices, wine and butter. Bring to the boil. Pour over chicken drumsticks. Leave to marinate for 30 minutes. Then bake in preheated oven at 200°C (400°F) for 30-35 minutes. Regularly turn drumsticks. When done, remove chicken from casserole. Keep warm. Thicken sauce with single cream and add lemon juice. Add chicken drumsticks to sauce and serve hot.

Mimoseneier

Zutaten

10 hartgek. Eier,
200 g Majonnaise,
1 D. Gänseleberpastete
   od. Kalbsleberwurst
1 Bund Petersilie
1 B. saure Sahne

Zubereitung

Die Eier der Länge nach halbieren u. das Eigelb herauslösen. Die Eiweißhälften mit Gänseleberpastete füllen u. dicht nebeneinander auf einer runden Platte anrichten. Majonnaise u. Sahne verrühren, über die Eier gießen, Eigelb durch ein Sieb streichen u. über die Majonnaise streuen. Die Eierplatte mit Petersilie umlegen.

Mimosa eggs (Mimoseneier)

Ingredients:

Metric		Imperial	
10	hardboiled eggs	10	hardboiled eggs
200 g	mayonnaise	8 oz	mayonnaise
1 tin	pâté de foie gras or calf's liver pâté	1 tin	pâté de foie gras or calf's liver pâté
1 bunch	parsley	1 bunch	parsley
200 ml	soured cream	3/8 pints	soured cream

Method:
Cut hardboiled eggs in half lengthwise. Remove yolks. Fill centre of the egg whites with pâté de foie gras or calf's liver pâte. Closely arrange them on a round serving platter. Mix mayonnaise and soured cream. Pour over the filled egg whites. Press the egg yolks through sieve and sprinkle over the mayonnaise mixture. Garnish with parsley.

Verlorene Eier auf Reissockel

Zutaten

1-2 Eier pro Person, 1 l. Wasser, etwas Essig, Salz u. Speck, 100g Schinken, Mehl, Tomatenmark, Pfeffer

Zubereitung

Wasser mit Essig u. Salz zum Kochen bringen. Eier einzeln in eine Suppenkelle vorsichtig aufschlagen u. ins Wasser gleiten lassen. 4 Min. kochen, vorsichtig herausnehmen. Speck auslassen, Wasser zugeben, Grieben herausnehmen, Schinken in Stck. schneiden u. 15-30 Min. mitkochen. Die Soße binden, über die Eier geben und mit Pfeffer u. Tomatenmark abschmecken.

Auf einem Reissockel anrichten.

"Lost" eggs on rice
(Verlorene Eier auf Reissockel)

Ingredients:

Metric		Imperial	
1-2	eggs (per person)	1-2	eggs (per person)
1 l	water	2 pints	water
	some vinegar		some vinegar
	salt		salt
	some bacon		some bacon
100 g	ham	4 oz	ham
	flour, tomatopurée, pepper		flour, tomatopurée, pepper

Method:
Mix water with vinegar and salt. Bring to the boil. Break eggs seperately into soup ladle and gently let slip into boiling water, one at a time. Dice bacon and fry in a pan. Add water and bring to the boil. Take off grieven. Dice ham and add into pan. Cook for 15-30 minutes. Thicken sauce with some flour while stirring constantly. Season to taste with pepper and tomatopurée. Pour over eggs.
Serve with rice.

Überbackene Eier

Zutaten
6-8 hartgekochte Eier
Bechamelsoße
geriebener Käse
Fettflöckchen

Zubereitung
In die gefettete Auflaufform die Hälfte der Soße geben, die halbierten Eier hineinlegen, den Rest der Soße auffüllen, mit geriebenem Käse überstreuen u. Fettflöckchen aufsetzen.
Im Backofen bei 225° 20-25 Min. goldgelb überbacken.
Mit Toast u. Blatt- oder Gemüsesalat als Vorspeise oder Abendgericht reichen.

Eggs in white sauce (Überbackene Eier)

Ingredients:

Metric		Imperial	
6-8	hardboiled eggs	6-8	hardboiled eggs
1 l	white sauce	2 pints	white sauce
	grated cheese		grated cheese
	flaked butter		flaked butter

Method:

Butter pie dish. Put half of the sauce in the dish. Cut hardboiled eggs in half lengthwise. Place in dish and cover with rest of the sauce. Sprinkle with grated cheese. Finally, spread some flaked butter over the cheese.
Bake in oven at 225°C (450°F) for 20-25 minutes until golden.
Serve with toast and lettuce or a mixed vegetable salad.

Let us eat and be merry.
Luke 15, 23

Lasset uns essen und fröhlich sein.
Lukas 15, 23

Vegetable and Potato Dishes

(Gemüse und Kartoffeln)

Überbackener Rosenkohl

Zutaten:
- 1 kg frischer **o d e r**
- 2 P. (600g) tiefgekühlter Rosenkohl
- 1 Zwiebel
- 1 Eßl. Butter oder Margarine
- 1 Teel. Aromat oder Fondor
- 125 g Emmentaler Käse
- 2 Eßl. Sahne oder Dosenmilch
- 1 Teel. Speisestärke

Zubereitung:

Frischen Rosenkohl putzen und waschen. Die Zwiebel schälen, würfeln und in Butter oder Margarine hellgelb andünsten. 1/2 Tasse Wasser, Aromat oder Fondor und frischen oder tiefgekühlten Rosenkohl dazugeben. Zudecken und in 25 Min. (frisch!) bzw. 15 Min. (tiefgekühlt!) gardünsten. Den Käse reiben, Sahne oder Dosenmilch mit Speisestärke verquirlen, zum Rosenkohl rühren und aufkochen. Den Rosenkohl auf eine feuerfeste Platte geben, mit dem Käse bestreuen und im heißen Backofen kurz überbacken. Mit Paprika bestäuben und mit Hackfleischsteaks (gibt es tiefgekühlt und fertig zum Braten) und Bratkartoffeln servieren.

Baked brussels sprouts
(Überbackener Rosenkohl)

Ingredients:

Metric		Imperial	
1 kg	fresh brussels sprouts	2 lb	fresh brussels sprouts
or 600 g	frozen brussels sprouts	or 24 oz	frozen brussels sprouts
1	onion	1	onion
1 T	butter or margarine	1 T	butter or margarine
125 ml	stock (cubes)	1/4 pint	stock (cubes)
125 g	Emmentaler (strong swiss cheese)	5 oz	Emmentaler (strong swiss cheese)
2 T	single cream	2 T	single cream
1 t	corn starch	1 t	corn starch

Method:

Clean and wash fresh brussels sprouts. Peel and dice onion. Braise in butter or margarine until yellow. Add stock and fresh or frozen brussels sprouts. Cover and let simmer for 25 minutes (fresh brussels sprouts) or 15 minutes (frozen brussels sprouts). Whisk single cream and corn starch. Add to brussels sprouts. Blend in and bring to the boil. Take off the heat. Grate cheese. Put brussels sprouts in a casserole and sprinkle with cheese. Bake in preheated oven until golden. Sprinkle with paprika and serve with meatballs and potatoes.

Gefüllter Blumenkohl

Zutaten:
- 1 gr. Blumenkohl
- 1/4 l Wasser
- Salz
- 200 g Gehacktes (halb und halb)
- Salz
- 1 Brötchen
- 1 EBl. Wasser
- Zitronengelb
- 30 g Fett
- 40 g Mehl
- 3/8 l Flüssigkeit
- Salz
- 25 g geriebener Käse
- Zitronensaft
- 1 Eigelb
- 1 Eischnee

Belag:
- geriebener Käse
- Fettflöckchen

Stuffed cauliflower (Gefüllter Blumenkohl)

Ingredients:

Metric		Imperial	
Cauliflower:			
1 large	cauliflower	1	large cauliflower
250 ml	water	1/2 pint	water
	salt		salt
Meat:			
100 g	minced pork	4 oz	minced pork
100 g	minced beef	4 oz	minced beef
	salt		salt
1	roll	1	roll
1 T	water	1 T	water
grated rind of untreated lemon		grated rind of untreated lemon	
Sauce:			
30 g	margarine	1 oz	margarine
40 g	flour	1 1/2 oz	flour
375 ml	stock	3/4 pints	stock
	salt		salt
25 g	grated cheese	1 oz	grated cheese
	lemon juice		lemon juice
1	egg (seperated)	1	egg (seperated)

Topping:
grated cheese, flaked butter

Zubereitung:

Den Blumenkohl garen, den Strunk herausschneiden, die Röschen müssen aber zusammenbleiben. In die Lücke und zwischen die Röschen die kräftig abgeschmeckte Fleischmasse drücken. Eine helle Grundsoße mit der Gemüsebrühe bereiten, mit dem Käse und Zitronensaft abschmecken, mit Eigelb legieren, den Eischnee unterheben und über den Blumenkohl in der Form füllen. Mit Käse bestreuen, Fettflöckchen aufsetzen und goldgelb backen.
Mit kleinen, in Fett geschwenkten Kartoffeln oder Röstkartoffeln reichen.

Einsetzen:
Mit dem Rost ⌐_⌐ untere Schiene.

Backen:
25 - 30 Min.   225° - 250°
 5 - 10 Min.   O

Method:

Steam whole cauliflower until done. Carefully remove core. The florets have to remain together. Soak roll in water. Squeeze out. Mix roll, meat and spices. Carefully stuff meat mixture between florets. Prepare white sauce as usual and blend in cheese and lemon juice. Add beaten egg yolk while stirring constantly. Fold in stiffly beaten egg white. Put stuffed cauliflower in a buttered pie dish. Cover with sauce. Sprinkle with cheese. Spread flaked butter over it. Put on the lowest shelf in a preheated oven (225°-250°C/450°-500°F) for 25-30 minutes until golden. Turn off heat. Leave cauliflower in closed oven for another 5-10 minutes. Serve with fried potatoes.

Weinsauerkraut mit Trauben

Zutaten:
- 1 Dose Sauerkraut (ca. 600g)
- 125 g helle Weintrauben
- 1 Zwiebel
- 1 Apfel
- 1 EBl. Schmalz oder Margarine
- 1/4 l Weißwein
- 1 Lorbeerblatt
- 1/2 Teel. weißer Pfeffer

Zubereitung:

Die Zwiebel schälen und in feine Ringe schneiden. Den Apfel schälen, vierteln, entkernen und in Scheiben schneiden. Schmalz oder Margarine im Gemüsetopf erhitzen, Zwiebel und Apfel darin hellgelb dünsten. Weißwein, Lorbeerblatt und Pfeffer hinzufügen und aufkochen. Das Sauerkraut schön locker mit einer Gabel hinzugeben, zudecken und 20 Min. kochen. Die Weintrauben kurz in kochendes Wasser legen, wieder herausnehmen und die Haut mit einem spitzen Messer abziehen. Die Trauben unter das Sauerkraut heben und kurz erhitzen.

Dazu Kartoffelpüree und knusprig gebratene Rostbratwürstchen oder Hähnchen-Röstl servieren.

Winesauerkraut with grapes
(Weinsauerkraut mit Trauben)

Ingredients:

METRIC		IMPERIAL	
600 g	fresh sauerkraut	24 oz	fresh sauerkraut
125 g	white grapes	5 oz	white grapes
1	onion	1	onion
1	apple	1	apple
1 T	lard or margarine	1 T	lard or margarine
250 ml	white wine	1/2 pint	white wine
1	bay leaf	1	bay leaf
1/2 t	white pepper	1/2 t	white pepper

Method:

Peel onion and slice. Peel apple, remove core and slice thinly. Heat lard or margarine in a saucepan. Braise onion and apple until golden brown. Add white wine, bay leaf and pepper. Bring to the boil. Loosen sauerkraut with a fork and add to saucepan. Cover grapes with boiling water to blanch, drain and remove skin with a sharp knife. Mix peeled grapes with sauerkraut. Serve with mashed potatoes and fried sausages or fried chicken.

Gefüllter Kohl

Zutaten: 2 Pfd. Wirsing
1 Pfd. Gehacktes
1 Ei
4 - 5 Zwiebacke
Gewürze, Salz

Zubereitung:
Den Wirsing in ganzen Blättern abkochen, Tuch in einen Durchschlag legen, Boden und Rand mit Wirsingblättern auslegen, schichtweise das mit Zwieback, Ei und Gewürzen gemischte Gehackte abwechselnd mit Kohlblättern einfüllen, Randblätter darüberklappen, Tuch mit einem Bindfaden zubinden und in Salzwasser 2 - 2½ Std. garkochen.
Von der Kochbrühe mit Mehl und etwas Butter eine weiße Schwitze herstellen und mit Zitrone und Kapern abschmecken.

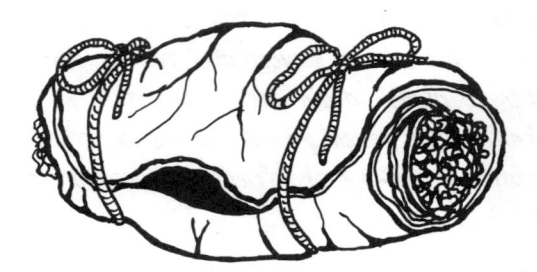

Stuffed Cabbage or Savoy (Gefüllter Kohl)

Ingredients:

Metric		Imperial	
1 kg	cabbage	2 lbs	cabbage
500 g	minced meat	1 lb	minced meat
1	egg	1	egg
4-5	unsweetened rusks	4-5	unsweetened rusks
seasoning, salt		seasoning, salt	

Method:

Separate cabbage leaves, wash and cook, uncovered in lightly salted water for about 10 minutes. Crush rusks, mix in egg, seasoning, salt and meat to make stuffing. Spread out damp muslin cloth in a shallow dish. Line cloth with some cabbage leaves. Spread some stuffing on cabbage leaves. Cover with some more cabbage leaves and spread some more stuffing over leaves. Repeat until stuffing and cabbage leaves are all in dish. Fold in outer leaves and cloth to form a large roll. Bind with thread. Simmer in lightly salted water for 2-2 1/2 hours. Remove from liquid and keep hot.

Heat some butter or margarine in a saucepan. Stir in some flour to make a smooth paste. Add cooking liquid, whilst constantly stirring. Season to taste. Blend in some lemon juice and capers. Serve with sliced cabbage roll.

Weiße Bohnen in Tomatensoße

Zutaten:
- 250 g weiße Bohnen
- 2 Zwiebeln
- 1 Knoblauchzehe
- 2 Eßl. Biskin
- 1/2 Tasse Rotwein
- 1 kl. Dose Tomatenmark
- etwas Instant-Bratensoße
- Salz, Pfeffer, Majoran

Zubereitung:

Bohnen im Einweichwasser aufsetzen und in 1 1/2 Std. weichkochen. Zwiebeln und Knoblauchzehe schälen, fein hacken und in Biskin goldbraun rösten. Rotwein und Tomatenmark hinzufügen, umrühren und aufkochen. Die gekochten Bohnen und 1-2 Tassen Kochwasser dazugeben und etwas Instant-Bratensoße hineinrühren. Aufkochen, mit Salz, Pfeffer und etwas Majoran (in den Händen fein zerreiben!) abschmecken. Nach Wunsch süß-sauer würzen; dafür 3-4 Eßl. Essig und etwas Zucker verwenden.

Mit gebratenem Speck und Weißbrot oder mit Bratwürsten (Art nach Wunsch) servieren.

Beans in Tomato Sauce
(Weiße Bohnen in Tomatensauce)

Ingredients:

Metric		Imperial	
250 g	kidney beans	10 oz	kidney beans
2	onions	2	onions
1	clove garlic	1	clove garlic
2 T	lard/margarine	2 T	lard/margarine
1/2 cup	red wine	1/2 cup	red wine
1 small can tomato puree		1 small can tomato puree	
some instant gravy powder		some instant gravy powder	
salt, pepper, marjoram		salt, pepper, marjoram	

Method:

Soak beans over night. Bring beans to the boil and simmer for approx. 1 1/2 hours. Chop onion and garlic and fry in lard until golden brown. Stir in red wine and tomato puree. Bring to the boil. Add beans and 1-2 cups of cooking fluid. Stir in gravy powder. Season with salt, pepper and marjoram.

Sauce can alternatively be served sweet-sour by adding 3-5 T vinegar and some sugar.

Serve with fried bacon or fried sausages and white bread.

Dicke Bohnen mit Speck

Zutaten:
- 2 P. à 300 g dicke Bohnen (tiefgekühlt)
- 1/4 l Fleischbrühe (Würfel)
- 1 Zweig / 1/2 Teel. Bohnenkraut
- 50 g Speck
- 1 EBl. Butter oder Margarine
- 2 Zwiebeln
- 1 EBl. Mehl
- 1/4 l Milch
- Salz, Pfeffer

Zubereitung:

Die gefrosteten dicken Bohnen in Fleischbrühe mit Bohnenkraut zugedeckt nach Vorschrift gardünsten. Unabhängig davon den Speck würfeln, bei schwacher Hitze glasig werden lassen, Fett und Zwiebelwürfel zugeben, Mehl beifügen und alles gelblich werden lassen. Mit kalter Milch und der heißen Bohnenflüssigkeit auffüllen, aufkochen, zu den Bohnen geben und diese noch ca. 5 Min. mit der Soße durchkochen. Das Gemüse zuletzt mit Salz und Pfeffer pikant abschmecken und sofort anrichten.

Broad Beans with Bacon
(Dicke Bohnen mit Speck)

Ingredients:

Metric		Imperial	
600 g	broad beans	1lb 4oz	broad beans
250 ml	stock	1/2 pint	stock
1/2 t	summer savory (chopped)	1/2 t	summer savory (chopped)
50 g	bacon	2 oz	bacon
1 T	butter or margarine	1 T	butter or margarine
2	onions	2	onions
1 T	flour	1 T	flour
250 ml	milk	1/2 pint	milk
salt, pepper		salt, pepper	

Method:

Put broad beans in saucepan, cover with stock and add summer savory. Cook until done (see cooking method on bean pack). While beans are cooking, dice and fry bacon until transparent. Sprinkle in flour, add chopped onions and fry whilst constantly stirring.. Blend in milk and hot bean stock. Allow to cook for a while. Continue stirring. Add beans to sauce and cook for another 5 min.. Season with salt and pepper to make a piquant sauce. Serve immediately.

Rotkohl mit Äpfeln

Zutaten:
- 1 kg Rotkohl
- 2 Zwiebeln
- 2 EBl. Schweineschmalz / Margarine
- 1/4 l Rotwein
- 2 EBl. Essig
- 6 Wacholderbeeren
- 1 Lorbeerblatt
- 3 Nelken
- Salz, Pfeffer
- 2 EBl. Honig / Johannisbeergelee/ Preiselbeerkompott
- 2 Äpfel
- etwas Mehl
- etwas Butter

Zubereitung:
Den Kohl putzen, vierteln, vom Strunk befreien und in feine Streifen hobeln. Die Zwiebeln schälen, würfeln und in Schmalz oder Margarine hellgelb dünsten. Den Kohl dazugeben und kurz mitdünsten. Rotwein und Essig hinzufügen, Wacholderbeeren, Nelken, Lorbeerblatt, etwas Salz und Pfeffer daruntermischen und den Kohl zugedeckt etwa 45 Min. kochen.

Red Cabbage with Apple
(Rotkohl mit Äpfeln)

Ingredients:

Metric		Imperial	
1 kg	red cabbage	2 lbs	red cabbage
2	onions	2	onions
2 T	lard or margarine	2 T	lard or margarine
250 ml	red wine	1/2 pint	red wine
2 T	vinegar	2 T	vinegar
6	juniper berries	6	juniper berries
1	bay leaf	1	bay leaf
3	cloves	3	cloves
salt, pepper		salt, pepper	
2 T	honey, redcurrant jelly or cranberry compôte	2 T	honey, redcurrant jelly or cranberry compôte
2	apples	2	apples
some flour, some butter		some flour, some butter	

Method:
Clean, quarter and core cabbage. Cut into small strips. Peel and dice onions. Melt lard or margarine in a large, heavy casserole. Add onions and fry until golden brown, then add cabbage. Cook gently. Stir in red wine, vinegar, juniper berries, cloves, bay leaf, some salt and pepper.

Honig, Johannisbeergelee oder Preiselbeerkompott darunterrühren und den Rotkohl abschmecken. Die Äpfel in Scheiben schneiden, entkernen, in Mehl wenden und in Butter goldgelb braten. Auf dem Rotkohl zu Hirschgulasch aus der Tiefkühltruhe und rohen Kartoffelklößen anrichten.

Cover and cook over medium heat for approx. 45 min. Add honey, redcurrant jelly or cranberry compôte to taste. Peel and core apples. Slice thinly, dust with flour then fry in butter until golden brown. Serve with venison stew (goulash) and potato dumplings (for recipe, see "Dumplings made of raw potatoes").

Brechbohnen mit Äpfeln u. Tomaten

Zutaten:
- 15 g durchwachsenen Speck
- 1 kleine Zwiebel
- 1 Tomate
- 50 g Äpfel
- 250 g Bohnen
- 1/4 l Wasser
- Salz
- Bohnenkraut
- Petersilie

Zubereitung:

Speck auslassen und kleingeschnittene Zwiebel glasig dünsten. Kleingeschnittene Tomate und Äpfel hinzufügen, etwas schmoren lassen und die gebrochenen Bohnen, Gewürze und Wasser zugeben. Ca. 20 Min. garen lassen.

French Beans with Apple and Tomato
(Brechbohnen mit Äpfeln u. Tomaten)

Ingredients:

Metric		Imperial	
15 g	bacon	1/2-3/4 oz bacon	
1	small onion	1	small onion
1	tomato	1 tomato	
50 g	apples	2 oz	apples
250 g	french beans (trimmed and cut)	1/2 lb	french beans (trimmed and cut)
250 ml	water	1/2 pint	water
salt, summer savory, parsley		salt, summer savory, parsley	

Method:
Fry diced bacon and chopped onion till transparent. Add chopped tomatoes and apples and leave to braise for a while. Stir in beans, chopped herbs and water. Season to taste. Simmer for about 20 min.

Käsespinat mit Pfannkuchen

Zutaten:
- 1 kg junger Spinat
- 50 g Räucherspeck
- 1 EßI. Butter oder Margarine
- 1 Zwiebel
- 1/2 Tasse Wasser
- Salz, Aromat oder Fondor
- 2 Ecken Sahne-Schmelzkäse
- 2 Eier
- 1/8 l Milch
- 2 EßI. Stärkemehl
- Muskat
- 250 g Mehl
- 3 - 4 Eier
- Salz
- ca. 1/2 l Milch
- Pflanzenöl zum Braten
- etwas geriebener Käse

Zubereitung:

Den Spinat gut verlesen und waschen, Speckwürfel in Fett auslassen, Zwiebelwürfel darin anschwitzen, Wasser, Salz, Aromat oder Fondor und den Spinat zugeben und zugedeckt ca. 5 Min. dünsten,

Cheese Spinach with Pancakes
(Käsespinat mit Pfannkuchen)

Ingredients:

Metric		Imperial	
1 kg	spinach	2-2 1/2 lbs	spinach
50 g	bacon	2 oz	bacon
1 t	butter or margarine	1 T	butter or margarine
1	onion	1	onion
1/2 cup	water	1/2 cup	water
salt, seasoning		salt, seasoning	
2 wedges	process cheese	2 wedges	process cheese
2	eggs	2	eggs
125 ml	milk	1/4 pint	milk
2 T	corn starch	2 T	corn starch
grated nutmeg		grated nutmeg	
250 g	flour	1/2 lb	flour
3-4	eggs	3-4	eggs
salt		salt	
500 ml	milk	1 pint	milk
margarine or cooking oil		margarine or cooking oil	
some grated cheese		some grated cheese	

danach mit einem Schneidstab gleich im Topf pürieren oder durch den Fleischwolf drehen. Den Käse mit den Eiern verrühren, Milch und Stärkemehl zugeben, die Masse unter den Spinat rühren und unter stetem Rühren nur einmal kurz aufkochen lassen.

Aus Mehl, Eiern, Salz und Milch einen Pfannkuchenteig bereiten, Pfannkuchen davon braten und auf einer feuerfesten Platte die Pfannkuchen immer mit einer Lage Spinat dazwischen aufschichten. Zuletzt Käse überstreuen, mit Fettflöckchen belegen und kurz überbacken.

Method:

Remove stems from spinach and wash. Braise diced bacon and onions in butter. Cook spinach for about 5 min. in seasoned water. Drain well and purée through sieve or vegetable mill.

Blend process cheese, eggs, milk, nutmeg and corn starch to make a paste. Stir in puréed spinach and bring to the boil whilst constantly stirring. Remove from heat.

To prepare pancake batter, mix flour, eggs, salt and milk well. Fry pancakes. Alternately arrange pancakes and spinach filling in a fireproof dish. Sprinkle on grated cheese and some flaked butter. Bake in moderate oven until a crust forms on the surface.

Grüne Bohnen mit Tomaten

Zutaten:
- 1 kg Brechbohnen o d e r
- 2 P. á 300g Tiefkühl-Brechbohnen
- 1/8 l Fleischbrühe (Würfel)
- 1 Zweig / 1/2 Teel. Bohnenkraut
- 100 g Räucherspeck
- 1 Teel. Butter oder Margarine
- 2 Zwiebeln
- 500 g Tomaten
- Salz, Pfeffer

Zubereitung:

Die Bohnen vorbereiten (frische Bohnen putzen, waschen und in Stücke brechen), in Fleischbrühe mit Bohnenkraut ca. 25-30 Min. dünsten. Unabhängig davon den Speck würfeln, in einer Pfanne auslassen. Fett zugeben, Zwiebelscheiben darin hellbraun werden lassen und die geschälten, in Spalten geschnittenen Tomaten beifügen. Die gegarten Bohnen abgießen, Speck, Zwiebeln und Tomaten untermischen und mit Salz und Pfeffer pikant abschmecken.

Als Beilage zu Steaks oder Braten reichen.

French Beans and Tomatoes
(Grüne Bohnen mit Tomaten)

Ingredients:

Metric		Imperial	
1 kg	french beans (trimmed and cut)	2-2 1/2 lbs	french beans (trimmed and cut)
125 ml	stock	1/4 pint	stock
sprig/1 1/2 t	summer savory	sprig/1 1/2 t	summer savory
100 g	bacon	4 oz	bacon
1 t	butter or margarine	1 t	butter or margarine
2	onions	2	onions
500 g	tomatoes	1 lb	tomatoes
salt, pepper		salt, pepper	

Method:

Cook beans and savory in stock for approx. 25 min. In the meantime, braise diced bacon and sliced onions until transparent. Blanch tomatoes and remove skin. Cut into wedges and add to bacon and onions. Mix in cooked beans. Season to taste. Serve with steak or roast.

Kartoffelknödel mit Pfiff

Zutaten: 1 P. Kartoffelknödelteig (halb und ha.
150 g alter Holland-Gouda
4 große Zwiebeln
60 g Butter

Zubereitung:

Kartoffelknödelmasse nach Vorschrift anrühren. Bevor die Masse fest wird, den geriebenen Gouda daruntergeben und aufquellen lassen. Wie auf der Packung beschrieben die Klöße formen und garen; gut abtropfen lassen und in eine Schüssel geben, die mit einem umgekehrten Teller ausgelegt ist. Zwiebeln in Ringe schneiden, in der Butter goldgelb braten und zu den Knödeln reichen.

Potato Dumplings with Pep
(Kartoffelknödel mit Pfiff)

Ingredients:

Metric		Imperial	
Potato Dumpling dough as on page 13			
150 g	strong cheese	6 oz	strong cheese
4	large onions	4	large onions
60 g	butter	2 1/2 oz	butter

Method:
Prepare potato dumpling dough as described on page 13. Mix in grated cheese. Leave for a while.
Continue preparing dumplings as described. Drain and put into serving dish. TIP: before putting into serving dish, place a plate of similar diameter upside-down on the bottom of dish. Fry onion rings until golden. Serve with dumplings.

Schusterpfanne

Zutaten: 75 g geräucherten durchw. Speck
3 Zwiebeln
750 g gekochte Kartoffeln
4 Debreciner oder Bratwürste
2 Gewürzgurken
1 rote Paprikaschote
1/2 Tasse Öl
Salz, Pfeffer (aus der Mühle)

Zubereitung:

Speck und Zwiebeln würfeln, gekochte Kartoffeln schälen und in Scheiben schneiden, Würstchen und Gurken in Scheiben, Paprikaschote in Streifen schneiden. Öl erhitzen und die Speckwürfel darin glasig werden lassen, Zwiebeln und Paprika dazugeben, kurz mitschwitzen. Restliche vorbereitete Zutaten nach und nach hinzufügen und unter mehrmaligem Wenden so lange braten, bis die Kartoffeln goldgelb geworden sind. Mit Salz und Pfeffer aus der Mühle würzen. Mit frisch geschnittenem Schnittlauch bestreuen und servieren.

Cobblers Casserole (Schusterpfanne)

Ingredients:

Metric		Imperial	
75 g	diced bacon	3 oz	diced bacon
3	onions	3	onions
750 g	potatoes boiled in their jackets	1 1/2 lbs	potatoes boiled in their jackets
4	frying sausages	4	frying sausages
1	large gherkin	1	large gherkin
1	red pepper	1	red pepper
1/2 cup	cooking oil	1/2 cup	cooking oil
salt, freshly ground pepper		salt, freshly ground pepper	

Method:

Remove jackets from potatoes. Slice potatoes, sausages and gherkin. Cut red pepper into thin strips. Heat oil and braise diced bacon until transparent. Add onions and red pepper. Allow to fry. Gradually add all other ingredients. Cook until potatoes turn golden brown. Season to taste. Before serving, sprinkle over some chopped chive.

**It is better to eat too much
than to prattle!**

*Lieber ein bißchen zuviel gegessen,
als ein bißchen zuviel geschwätzt!*

Casseroles and Soufflés

(Aufläufe und Mehlspeisen)

Quarkauflauf m. Äpfeln

Zutaten

3 Eigelb, 125g Zucker, 500g Quark, Zitronengelb, 75g Grieß. 1/2 P. Backp., 500g Äpfel, 3 Eischnee.

Zubereitung

Eigelb u. Zucker schaumig rühren, Quark, Zitronengelb u. Grieß mit Backp. vermengt zusetzen. Äpfel schälen, in feine Scheiben schneiden, in die Quarkmasse geben u. zuletzt den steifen Eischnee unterheben. In eine gefettete Auflaufform füllen und bei 200 - 210° 35 - 40 Min. backen.
Auf 0° noch 5 - 10 Min.
Man kann auch andere Obstsorten verwenden.

Curd Soufflé with Apples
(Quarkauflauf mit Äpfeln)

Ingredients:

Metric		Imperial	
3	eggs (seperated)	3	eggs (seperated)
125 g	sugar	5 oz	sugar
500 g	curd (smooth cottage cheese)	1 lb	curd (smooth cottage cheese)
grated rind of one untreated lemon		grated rind of one untreated lemon	
75 g	semolina	3 oz	semolina
1/2	packet baking powder	1/2	packet baking powder
500 g	cooking apples	1 lb	cooking apples

Method:

Beat egg yolks and sugar until creamy. Add curd and grated rind of one lemon. Mix semolina and baking powder together and add to egg mixture. Peel apples and cut into thin slices. Blend into curd mixture. Fold in stiffly beaten egg whites. Fill mixture into a buttered soufflé dish and bake in a preheated oven at 200-210°C (400° F) for 35 - 40 minutes. Turn off the oven (0°). Leave the soufflé in the oven for another 5-10 minutes. Instead of apples, other fruits can be used (cherries, pineapple, etc.)

Schlummerapfel

Zutaten

8 Eßl. Milch, 100g Butter, 150g kern. Haferflocken, 125g Zucker, 2 Eigelb, 2 Eischnee, 250g Quark, 1 Zitrone, 2-3 Eßl. Rum, 1 Messersp. Backpulver, 4-5 mittelgroße Äpfel, etwas Konfitüre

Zubereitung

Haferflocken in Milch 10-15 Min. quellen lassen. Butter, Zucker u. Eigelb schaumig rühren, Quark u. Zitronensaft zugeben, mit Flocken u. Backp. vermischen, Eischnee unterziehen. Äpfel schälen, Kerngehäuse ausstechen, die Hälfte des Teiges in die gefettete Auflaufform geben, Äpfel daraufsetzen, mit Konfi=

Slumbering apple (Schlummerapfel)

Ingredients:

Metric		Imperial	
8 T	milk	8 T	milk
100 g	butter	4 oz	butter
150 g	oat flakes	6 oz	oat flakes
125 g	sugar	5 oz	sugar
2 eggs (seperated)		2 eggs (seperated)	
250 g	curd (smooth cottage cheese)	1/2 lb	curd (smooth cottage cheese)
1	lemon	1	lemon
2-3 T	rum	2-3 T	rum
1/2 t	baking powder	1/2 t	baking powder
4-5 medium-sized apples		4-5 medium-sized apples	
some teaspoons jam or jelly		some teaspoons jam or jelly	

Method:

Soak oat flakes in milk for 10-15 minutes. Whisk butter, sugar and egg yolks until creamy. Add curd and lemon juice. Then add baking powder and soaked oat flakes. Mix well. Fold in stiffly beaten egg whites.

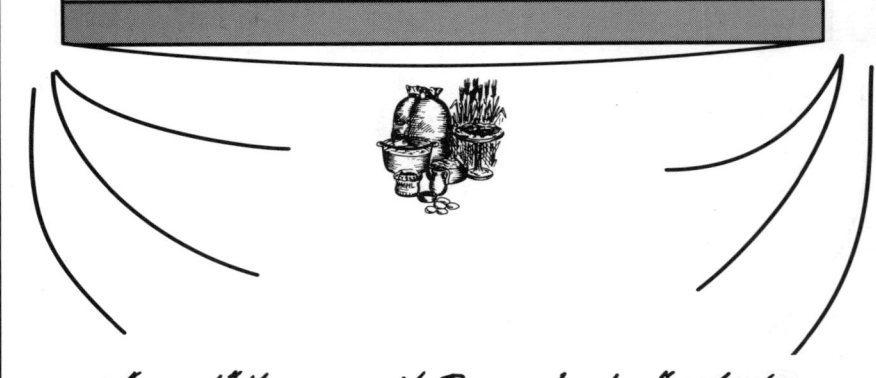

türe füllen, mit Rum beträufeln, Rest des Teiges zwischen die Äpfel verteilen.
Bei 200° 40 Min. backen
Nach Belieben Vanillesosse dazu reichen.

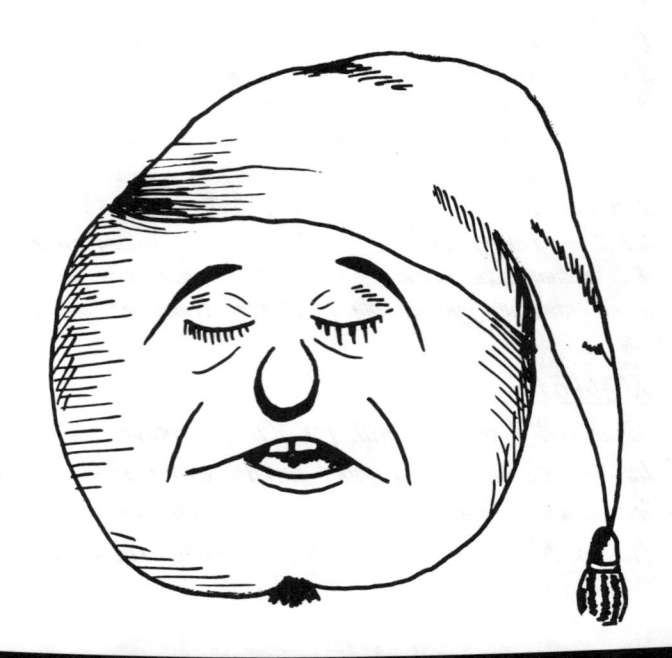

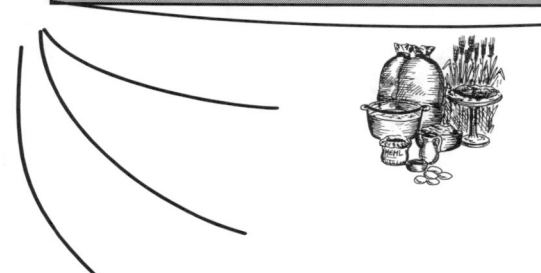

Peel apples and remove core. Put half of curd mixture in a buttered soufflé dish. Arrange apples on it. Fill the apples with jam or jelly, sprinkle with rum. Spread rest of curd mixture over and around the apples. Bake for 40 minutes in a preheated oven at 200°C (400°F).
Serve with vanilla sauce/custard (optional).

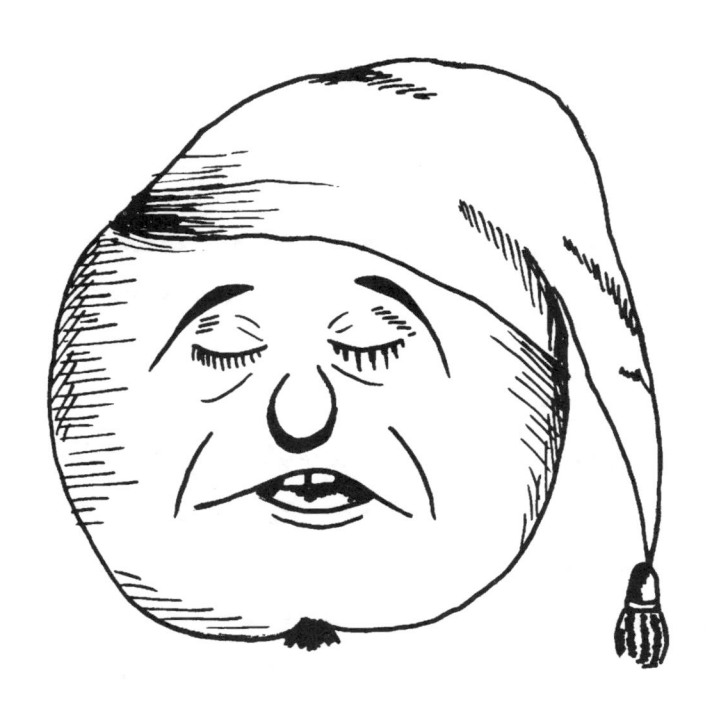

Apfel-Brot-Auflauf

Zutaten

3 Brötchen, 0,2 l koch. Milch,
40 g Zucker, 30g flüssige Butter,
250g saure Äpfel 400g Magerquark,
2 Eigelb, 1 P. Van.-Zucker,
30g Zucker, 1 Pr. Salz, 2 Eiweiß,
1 Van.-Pudding, Saft einer Zitrone,
20g Butter für die Form,
30g Butterflöckchen, 2 EBl. Zucker,

Für die Soße: 2 Eer, 80g Zucker,
1/4 l. Apfelwein

Zubereitung

Brötchen grob würfeln, m. koch. Milch übergießen. Zucker u. Butter darübergeben u. 15 Min. ziehen lassen. Die kleingeschnittenen Äpfel unter die Brötchen masse

Apple-Bread-Pie
(Apfel-Brot-Auflauf)

Ingredients:

Metric		Imperial	
3	rolls	3	rolls
200 ml	scalded milk	1/4-1/2	pints scalded milk
40 g	sugar	1 1/2 oz	sugar
30 g	melted butter	1 oz	melted butter
250 g	sour apples	1/2 lb	sour apples
400 g	low fat curd	16 oz	low fat curd
2	eggs (seperated)	2	eggs (seperated)
1/2 t	vanilla extract	1/2 t	vanilla extract
1	pinch of salt	1	pinch of salt
1	packet custard powder (50 g)	1	packet custard powder (2 oz)
juice of one lemon		juice of one lemon	
20 g	fat to grease tin	1 oz	fat to grease tin
30 g	flaked butter	1 1/2 oz	flaked butter
2 T	sugar	2 T	sugar

For sauce:

2	eggs	2	eggs
80 g	sugar	3 oz	sugar
250 ml	wine (apple-cider if available)	1/2 pint	wine (apple-cider if available)

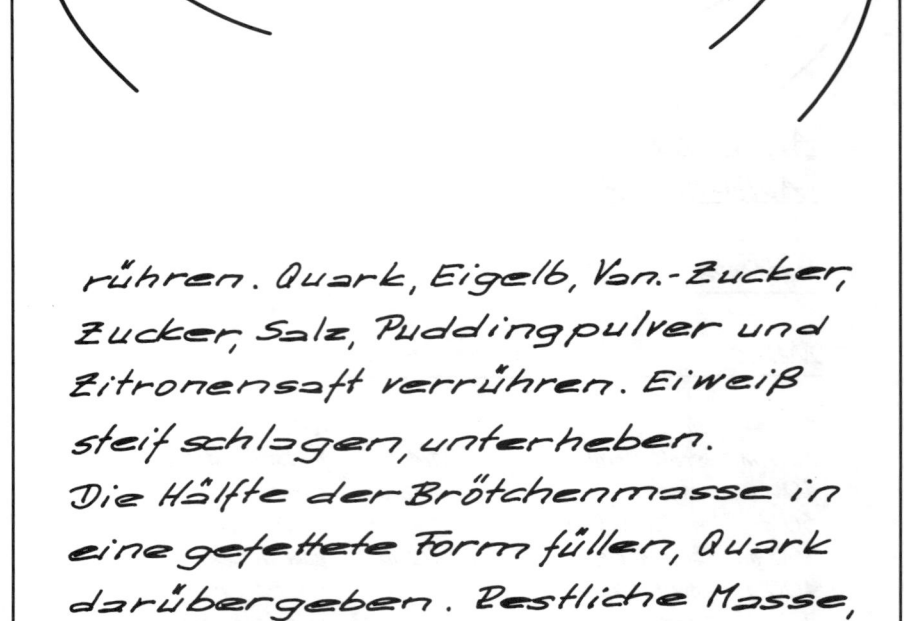

rühren. Quark, Eigelb, Van.-Zucker, Zucker, Salz, Puddingpulver und Zitronensaft verrühren. Eiweiß steif schlagen, unterheben.
Die Hälfte der Brötchenmasse in eine gefettete Form füllen, Quark darübergeben. Restliche Masse, Butterflöckchen u. dann Zucker darüber verteilen.
Alles bei 220° 45 Min. backen.

Für die Soße alle Zutaten in einem Topf verrühren. Bei geringer Temperatur oder im Wasserbad solange schlagen, bis die Masse dick wird.

Method:

Cut rolls in half and dice. Cover with scalded milk, sugar and butter. Soak for 15 min. Peel, core and slice apples. Mix with soaked bread. Mix curd, egg yolks, vanilla extract, sugar, salt, custard powder and lemon juice. Beat egg whites until stiff. Fold into curd mixture. Put half of the bread mixture in a buttered fireproof dish. Cover with curd mixture. Spread rest of the bread mixture on top. Sprinkle with flaked butter and sugar. Bake in preheated oven at 220°C (450° F) for 45 min.

For sauce:
Mix all ingredients in the top of a double saucepan. Set over hot, not boiling water. Stir over low heat until the mixture thickens.

Kirsch-Schwarzbrot-Auflauf

Zutaten

350g Vollkornbrot, 1/2 l Rotwein, oder Obstsaft, 100g Schokolade, 150g Zucker, 3 Eigelb, 1 P. Van.-Zucker, 1 Messersp. gem. Nelken, 1 Pr. Salz, 100g ger. Haselnüsse, 2 Eßl. Haferflocken, 1 Gl. Sauerkirschen, etwas Salz, 3 Eiweiß, 20g Butter

Für die Eischaumhaube:
1 Eiweiß, 3 Teel. Zucker, 1 Eigelb,
Außerdem: 1 Tasse Kirschsaft, 1 Tasse Zucker, 1 Eiweiß

Zubereitung

Das gewürfelte Brot 15 Min. in dem Rotwein einweichen. Inzwischen die Schokolade reiben. Eigelb, Zucker u. Van.-Zucker schaumig-

Cherry and Wholemeal Bread Pie (Kirsch-Schwarzbrot-Auflauf)

Ingredients:

Metric		Imperial	
350 g	wholemeal bread	14 oz	wholemeal bread
125 ml	red wine or fruit juice	1/4 pint	red wine or fruit juice
100 g	chocolate	4 oz	chocolate
150 g	sugar	6 oz	sugar
3	eggs (seperated)	3	eggs (seperated)
1/2 t	vanilla extract	1/2 t	vanilla extract
1	pinch of ground cloves	1	pinch of ground cloves
1	pinch of salt	1	pinch of salt
100 g	grated hazelnuts	4 oz	grated hazelnuts
2 T	oat flakes	2 T	oat flakes
1 jar	sour cherries	1 jar	sour cherries
20 g	butter	1 oz	butter

For the topping:
1	egg (seperated)	1	egg (seperated)
3 t	sugar	3 t	sugar

For the sauce:
1 cup	of cherry juice	1 cup	of cherry juice
1 cup	of sugar	1 cup	of sugar
1	egg white	1	egg white

schlagen. Nelken, Salz, Nüsse u. Schokolade zufügen. Die Eimasse, Haferflocken u. Kirschen unter die Brotmasse rühren. Zum Schluß die mit etwas Salz steifgeschlagenen Eiweiß unterheben.

Alles in eine gebutterte Form füllen und bei 200° etwa 25 Minuten backen.

Inzwischen Eiweiß steif schlagen, Zucker zufügen u. weiterschlagen, bis sich der Zucker gelöst hat. Eigelb unterrühren. Die Eimasse auf den Auflauf streichen, restl. Kirschen darüber verteilen. Alles noch mal 15 Min. weiterbacken bis die Eihaube goldgelb ist.

Für den Kirschsaft-Schaum Saft, Zucker u. Eiweiß schaumig schlagen.

Sofort servieren!

Method:

Soak diced bread for 15 min. in red wine (fruit juice). Grate chocolate. Beat yolks, sugar and vanilla extract until creamy. Add ground cloves, salt, nuts and chocolate. Drain cherries. Mix egg mixture, oat flakes and 2/3 of the cherries with the bread mixture. Finally fold in stiffly beaten egg whites. Put the mixture into a buttered fireproof dish. Bake in preheated oven at 200°C (400°F) for about 25 min. In the meantime, beat the egg white for the topping until fluffy. Add sugar and keep on whisking until sugar has dissolved. Then blend in yolk. Spread the egg mixture over the pie and garnish with the rest of the cherries. Bake for another 15 min. until topping is golden brown.

For the cherry sauce:
Beat juice, sugar and egg white until light and creamy. Serve immediately.

Deftiger Pilzauflauf

Zutaten

1000g Pellkartoffeln, Salz, Pfeffer,
50g mag. Speck, 200g Zwiebel,
1000g Pilze od. 1 Große Dose Pilze,
¼l saure Sahne, 10g Mehl,
Salz, Pfeffer, Rosmarin,
Thymian, geh. Petersilie,
2 Scheiben Käse, 2 Tomaten,
20g Margarine evtl. 20g Speck

Zubereitung

Die gek. Kartoffeln in Scheiben schneiden u. leicht würzen. In einer Pfanne Speckwürfel auslassen, Zwiebelringe darin glasig dünsten und die Pilze hinzufügen, so lange schmoren, bis die Flüssigkeit fast verdampft ist. Mit in saurer Sahne verquirltem Mehl binden u. alles

Spicy Mushroom Pie
(Deftiger Pilzauflauf)

Ingredients:

Metric		Imperial	
1 kg	potatoes	2 lbs	potatoes
	salt, pepper		salt, pepper
50 g	lean bacon	2 oz	lean bacon
200 g	onions	8 oz	onions
1 kg	mushrooms	2 lb	mushrooms
or one large can of mushrooms		or one large can of mushrooms	
(or the equivalent in weight of fresh mushrooms)			
250 ml	soured cream	1/2 pint	soured cream
1 level T	flour	1 level T	flour
	salt, pepper, rosemary, thyme, chopped parsley		salt, pepper, rosemary, thyme, chopped parsley
2 slices	cheese	2 slices	cheese
2	tomatoes	2	tomatoes
20 g	flaked margarine or	1 oz	flaked margarine or
20 g	rashers of bacon	1 oz	rashers of bacon

pikant abschmecken.
Abwechselnd Kartoffeln u. Pilze in eine Auflaufform schichten. Obenauf mit vier halben Käsescheiben u. mit abgezogenen, halbierten Tomaten belegen. Margarineflöckchen u. evtl. Speckstreifen auf den Auflauf geben u. alles im vorgeheizten Backofen bei 200-225° 30-40 Minuten überbacken.
Beilage: Salat

Method:

Boil potatoes until done. Drain, remove skin and slice. Season lightly with salt and pepper. Dice bacon and braise in a pan. Peel and dice onions. Add to bacon and braise until fluid is reduced. Mix flour and soured cream. Add to saucepan and blend in well. Season to taste with salt, pepper, rosemary, thyme and chopped parsley until spicy. Put potatoes and mushrooms in a buttered fireproof dish, alternating layer by layer. Cover with slices of cheese and flaked margarine or rashers of bacon. Bake in preheated oven at 200-225°C (400-450°F) for 30-40 min.
Serve with a salad of your choice.

Rhabarber-Auflauf

Zutaten

500g Rhabarber, 1 P. Van.-Zucker,
50g Zucker, 1/8 l Wasser,
20g Butter f. die Form,
100g Toastbrot, (5 Scheiben)
25g flüssige Butter,
150g zerkl. Kokosmakronen,
3 Eigelb, 60g Zucker, Salz,
1 P. Van.-Zucker, 3 Eiweiß,
1/8 l Milch

Für die Soße: 1/8 - 1/4 l Rhabarbersaft, etw. kalt. Wasser
1-2 Teel. Speisestärke
2 EBl. Crème fraîche

Zubereitung

Rhabarber in etwa 2½ cm breite
Stücke schneiden. Van.-Zucker

Rhubarb-pie (Rhabarber-Auflauf)

Ingredients:

Metric		Imperial	
500 g	rhubarb	1 lb	rhubarb
1/2 t	vanilla extract	1/2 t	vanilla extract
50 g	sugar	2 oz	sugar
125 ml	water	1/4 pint	water
20 g	grease for pie dish	1 oz	grease for pie dish
100 g	toast bread (5 slices)	4 oz	toast bread (5 slices)
25 g	melted butter	1 oz	melted butter
150 g	coconut macaroones	6 oz	coconut macaroones
3	eggs (seperated)	3	eggs (seperated)
60 g	sugar	2 oz	sugar
	salt		salt
1/2 t	vanilla extract	1/2 t	vanilla extract
125 ml	milk	1/4 pint	milk

For the sauce:
125-250ml	rhubarb-juice	1/4-1/2 pint	rhubarb-juice
some cold water		some cold water	
1-2 t	corn starch	1-2 t	corn starch
2 T	double cream	2 T	double cream

und Zucker in Wasser aufkochen, Rhabarberstücke hineingeben u. einmal aufkochen. Dann den Topf zugedeckt beiseite stellen u. abkühlen lassen. Eine feuerfeste Form ausfetten, gewürfeltes Toastbrot hineingeben u. mit Butter beträufeln. Kokosmakronen darüber verteilen.

Eigelb m. Zucker, Van.-Zucker u. Salz schaumig schlagen. Eiweiß zu Schnee schlagen, mit der Eigelbmasse vermischen. Dann mit Milch aufgießen u. gut durchschlagen. Abgetropften Rhabarber über die Makronen geben u. die Eiermilch darübergießen.

Bei 200° ca. 20 Min. backen. Den Rhabarbersaft aufkochen, mit Stärke binden u. mit Crème fraîche verfeinern.

Method:

Prepare rhubarb and slice. Bring water, and sugar to the boil. Add rhubarb pieces. Bring to the boil again. Cover and remove from heat. Leave to cool. Grease a pie dish, put in diced bread. Pour over melted butter. Crush coconut macaroones and sprinkle over buttered bread. Beat yolks with sugar, vanilla extract and salt until creamy. Whisk egg whites until fluffy. Blend in with the yolk cream. Add milk and beat well. Drain rhubarb pieces and add into pie dish. Cover rhubarb with egg mixture. Bake in pre-heated oven at 200°C (400°F) for about 20 minutes. Bring rhubarb-juice to the boil. Mix corn starch with a bit of water to make a thick paste. Gradually add to boiling juice, stirring constantly. Blend in double cream. Serve hot.

Kirschauflauf

Zutaten

½ l Milch, 1 Pr. Salz, 1 Van.-Zucker, 100g Grieß, 65g Butter, 100g Zucker, 4 Eigelb, abger. Zitronenschale, 4 Eiweiß, 500g gek. Kirschen

Zubereitung

Grieß mit Milch, Salz u. Van.-Zucker unter Rühren zum Kochen bringen u. 5 Min. schwach weiterkochen. Butter u. Zucker schaumig rühren Eigelb u. Zitronenschale untermischen, Grießbrei unterziehen, Eischnee unterheben. Auflaufform fetten u. mit Grieß ausstreuen, abgetropfte Kirschen hineingeben u. Grießmasse daraufüllen.
Bei 200° ca. 25 Min. backen.
Kirschsaft binden u. dazugeben.

Cherry Pie (Kirschauflauf)

Ingredients:

Metric		Imperial	
500ml	milk	1 pint	milk
1 pinch of salt		1 pinch of salt	
1/2 t	vanilla extract	1/2 t	vanilla extract
100 g	semolina	4 oz	semolina
65 g	butter	2 1/2 oz	butter
100 g	sugar	4 oz	sugar
4	eggs (seperated)	4	eggs (seperated)
grated rind of one untreated lemon		grated rind of one untreated lemon	
1 large jar cherries		1 large jar cherries	

Method:

Mix semolina, milk, vanilla extract. Bring to the boil while stirring constantly. Reduce heat and allow to simmer for about 5 min. Whisk butter amd sugar until creamy, add yolks and lemon rind. Beat well.
Add semolina mixture and stiffly beaten egg whites. Grease pie dish and sprinkle with some semolina. Drain cherries and put into pie dish. Cover with semolina mixture. Bake at 200°C (400°F) for about 25 min. Bring cherry-sauce to the boil. Mix corn starch with some water to make a thick paste. Gradually add to boiling juice, stirring constantly.
Serve with the pie.

Spinat-Auflauf

Zutaten

200g Makkaroni, Salz, 2 Eier,
600g Rahm-Spinat, 20g Butter,
250g Champignons, Pfeffer,
 50g geriebenen Käse

Zubereitung

Makkaroni 10 Min. in Salzwasser garkochen, abgießen u. sofort in den verquirlten Eiern wenden. Spinat nach Vorschrift zubereiten u. etwas einkochen lassen. Pilze in Butter dünsten u. würzen.
Auflaufform fetten, 2/3 der Makkaroni einlegen, Spinat, Pilze, restl. Makkaroni u. Käse darauf schichten.
15-20 Min. im vorgeheizten Ofen bei 225° überbacken.

Spinach Pie (Spinat-Auflauf)

Ingredients:

Metric		Imperial	
200 g	maccaroni	8 oz	maccaroni
	salt		salt
2	eggs	2	eggs
600 g	frozen spinach	1 1/4 lb	frozen spinach
20 g	butter	1 oz	butter
250 g	mushrooms	1/2 lb	mushrooms
	pepper, salt		pepper, salt
50 g	grated cheese	2 oz	grated cheese

Method:

Boil maccaroni in salted water for about 10 min. until done. Drain and mix with whisked eggs. Prepare spinach according to cooking instructions. Braise mushrooms and season to taste. Butter pie dish. Put 2/3 of the maccaroni into dish. Spread spinach over the maccaroni and put mushrooms on top. Cover with the rest of the maccaroni. Sprinkle with grated cheese. Bake in preheated oven at 225°C (450°F) for 15-20 min.

Pflaumen-Kartoffel-Auflauf

Zutaten

Für den Kartoffelteig:

600g am Vortage gekochte Salz-Kartoffeln,
60g Crème fraiche, 1/4 Teel. Salz,
etwas abgerieb. Muskatnuss,
3 Teel. Zucker, 3 Eiweiß

Außerdem:

25g Butter f. d. Form, 2 Eßl. Zucker,
2 Eßl. Semmelbrösel,
600g frische Pflaumen, od. 1 Glas,
50g Crème fraiche,
3 Eßl. groß geh. Haselnüsse,
40g Butterflöckchen, Zucker, Zimt,
2 Teel. Speisestärke

Zubereitung

Durchgepreßte Kartoffeln mit den Zutaten f. d. Kartoffelteig und

Plum Potatoe Pie
(Pflaumen-Kartoffel-Auflauf)

Ingredients:

Metric		Imperial	

For the potatoe dough:
600 g	cooked potatoes	24 oz	cooked potatoes
60 g	double cream	2 1/2 oz	double cream
1 pinch	salt	1 pinch	salt
	some grated nutmeg		some grated nutmeg
3 t	sugar	3 t	sugar
3	egg whites	3	egg whites

Topping:
25 g	grease for the pie dish	1 oz	grease for the pie dish
2 T	sugar	2 T	sugar
2 T	bread crumbs	2 T	bread crumbs
600 g	fresh plums or	24 oz	fresh plums or
1	large jar plum compôte	1	large jar plum compôte
50 g	double cream	2 oz	double cream
3 T	chopped hazelnuts	3 T	chopped hazelnuts
40 g	flaked butter	1 1/2 oz	flaked butter
	sugar, cinnamon		sugar, cinnamon

das steifgeschlagenen Eiweiß verrühren. Eine feuerfeste Form fetten u. ausbröseln. Die Hälfte der Kartoffelmasse hineingeben, mit den Pflaumen bedecken. Creme fraiche u. Nüsse darüber verteilen. Dann alles mit der restlichen Kartoffelmasse bedecken. Butterflöckchen darübergeben.
Bei 220° ca. 35 Min. backen.

Zucker u. Zimt dazu reichen.

Method:

Mix mashed potatoes with double cream, salt, sugar and stiffly beaten egg whites. Butter pie dish and sprinkle with bread crumbes. Put half of the potato mixture in the dish. Cover with plums. Spread double cream and nuts over the plums. Cover with rest of potato mixture. Sprinkle with flaked butter. Bake at 220°C (450°F) for approx. 35 min.
Serve with sugar and ground cinnamon.

Sauerkrautauflauf

Zutaten

1 Gl. Pfifferlinge, 1 Zwiebel,
60g Schmalz, 500g Sauerkraut,
¼ l Apfelwein oder Apfelsaft,
Salz, Pfeffer, 1 gr. Kartoffel,
3 Mettwürstchen

Für die Kartoffelhaube:

750g Kartoffeln, 125g Goudakäse,
4 Eier, Salz, Pfeffer, ger. Muskatnuß

Zubereitung

Pfifferlinge abgießen, Zwiebel würfeln,
im Schmalz andünsten u. Sauerkraut
zufügen. Mit Apfelwein aufgießen und
mit Salz u. Pfeffer würzen.
Zugedeckt etwa 20 Min. dünsten.
Pilze zugeben u. alles mit geriebener
Kartoffel binden. Die Hälfte des
Krauts in eine gefettete Auflauf=

Sauerkraut Casserole (Sauerkrautauflauf)

Ingredients:

Metric		Imperial	
1 jar	chanterelles	1 jar	chanterelles
1	onion	1	onion
60 g	lard	2 1/2 oz	lard
500 g	sauerkraut	1 lb	sauerkraut
250 ml	cider or apple juice	1/2 pint	cider or apple juice
	salt, pepper		salt, pepper
1 large	potato	1 large	potato
3	Bologna sausages	3	Bologna sausages

For the topping:

750 g	potatoes	1 1/2 lb	potatoes
125 g	Gouda (Dutch cheese)	4 oz	Gouda (Dutch cheese)
4	eggs	4	eggs
salt, pepper, grated nutmeg		salt, pepper, grated nutmeg	

Method:

Drain chanterelles. Peel and dice onions, braise in lard. Add sauerkraut and cider (or juice).

form füllen. Die Würstchen klein
schneiden u. mit dem restl. Kraut
abdecken.
Kartoffeln für die Haube grob
raspeln, Käse reiben, mit Eiern
und Gewürzen mischen und auf das
Kraut verteilen.
Im vorgeheizten Backofen
bei 175° etwa 45 Min. garen.

Season with salt and pepper to taste. Cover and simmer for about 20 min. Add chanterelles and thicken with peeled, grated potato. Put half of the sauerkraut mixture in a greased pie dish. Cut sausages into thin slices. Spread over the sauerkraut mixture. Cover with rest of sauerkraut.

For topping:
Peel and grate potatoes. Mince cheese. Mix potatoes and cheese with eggs and spices. Spread over the sauerkraut.
Bake in preheated oven for about 45 min.
(175°C /350°F).

Schinkenreis

Zutaten
250g Reis, 80g Butter, 4 Eier, 250g Schinken, Salz

Zubereitung
Den Reis in Salzwasser garkochen. Auf ein Sieb schütten u. kalt überspülen. Butter u. Eier schaumig rühren u. mit dem Schinken unter den Reis mischen. In eine Form geben und im vorgeheizten Backofen bei ca 200° goldgelb überbacken.
Dazu reicht man Salat.

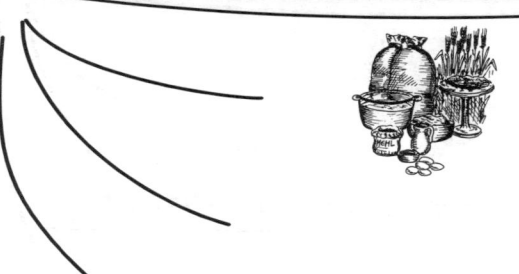

Ham and Rice Dish (Schinkenreis)

Ingredients:

Metric		Imperial	
250 g	rice	1/2 lb	rice
80 g	butter	3 oz	butter
4	eggs	4	eggs
250 g	ham	1/2 lb	ham
	salt		salt

Method:
Boil rice in salted water until done. Drain and rinse with cold water. Beat butter and eggs until creamy. Evenly mix all ingredients with each other. Put mixture in a buttered pie dish and bake in pre-heated oven at 200°C (400°F). Serve with a salad of your choice.

Rotkohl in gebackenem Fischring

Zutaten

750g Fischfleisch, 125g Margarine, 200g Weißbrot, Milch, Salz, Gewürze, Zitronensaft.

Zubereitung

Das rohe Fleisch durch einen Wolf drehen. Die Fleischmasse mit dem in Milch eingeweichten u. ausgedrückten Weißbrot, mit Margarine, Salz, Gewürzen u. Zitronensaft gut vermischen. Den Fischteig in eine gefettete u. mit Paniermehl ausgestreute Kranzform füllen u. im Ofen 20 Min. backen. In den gestürzten Ring kann man geschmorten Rotkohl geben, auch Rotkrautsalat eignet sich sehr gut.
Kartoffelschnee od. Kartoffelbrei vervollständigen das schmackhafte Gericht.

Red Cabbage in Ring of Baked Fish
(Rotkohl in gebackenem Fischring)

Ingredients:

Metric		Imperial	
750 g	fish filet	1 1/2 lb	fish filet
125 g	margarine	4 oz	margarine
200 g	white bread	7 oz	white bread
	milk		milk
	salt, seasoning		salt, seasoning
	lemon juice		lemon juice

Method:

Mince fish filet. Soak white bread in milk. Squeeze out excess milk. Blend all ingredients well. Grease a baking-ring and sprinkle with bread crumbs. Put fish mixture into baking-ring. Bake in preheated oven at moderate heat for about 20 min. Prepare red cabbage as usual. When fish ring is done, turn out onto a serving platter. Put red cabbage into hollow of ring. Serve with mashed potatoes.

Kartoffelauflauf m. Hackfleisch

Zutaten

8-10 Kartoffeln, 2 Zwiebeln, Salz,
400 g gemischtes Hackfleisch,
schw. Pfeffer, Zwiebelpulver,
2 Pellkartoffeln, 1/8 l Kaffeesahne,
1 Ei, Fett f. d. Form, 100 g. ger. Gouda,
2 Eßl. Kaffeesahne

Zubereitung

Kartoffeln u. Zwiebeln in dicke Scheiben schneiden. Hackfleisch mit Gewürzen, zerquetschten Pellkartoffeln, 1/8 l Sahne u. dem Ei mischen. Zu einem lockeren Teig verrühren. Auflaufform einfetten, mit der Hälfte der Kartoffel- u. Zwiebelscheiben auslegen, mit Salz u. Pfeffer würzen. Hackfleisch darauf breiten, mit den restl. Kartoffel- u. Zwiebel=

Minced Meat and Potato Pie
(Kartoffelauflauf mit Hackfleisch)

Ingredients:

Metric		Imperial	
8-10	potatoes	8-10	potatoes
2	onions	2	onions
	salt		salt
200 g	minced pork	7 oz	minced pork
200 g	minced beef	7 oz	minced beef
	black pepper		black pepper
	onion powder		onion powder
2	boiled potatoes	2	boiled potatoes
125 ml	unsweetened evaporated milk	1/4 pint	unsweetened evaporated milk
1	egg	1	egg
	grease for pie dish		grease for pie dish
100 g	grated Gouda (Dutch cheese)	4 oz	grated Gouda (Dutch cheese)
2 T	unsweetened evaporated milk	2 T	unsweetened evaporated milk

scheiben bedecken, würzen.
Sahne darauf verteilen u. 50g Käse
überstreuen. Form schließen u. im
vorgeheizten Ofen bei 225°
30 Min backen. Danach den rest=
lichen Käse überstreuen und
weitere 20 Min. backen.
Dazu reicht man: Tomaten=
soße, Zuckererbsen oder
Rohkostsalat.

Method:

Peel potatoes and onions and cut into thick slices. Peel and mash boiled potatoes. Mix minced meat, spices, mashed potatoes, milk and egg. Grease pie dish. Put in half of the potato and onion slices. Season with salt and pepper. Add meat mixture. Spread over evenly. Cover with rest of the potato and onion slices. Season with salt and pepper. Pour 2 T unsweetened evaporated milk over mixture. Cover pie dish and bake in preheated oven at 225°C (450°F) for about 30 min. Sprinkle rest of the cheese over pie and bake for another 20 min.

Serve with tomato sauce, peas or salad of your choice.

Schwalbennester

Zutaten

500g Gehacktes halb u. halb
1 Brötchen
1 Ei
1 Zwiebel
Salz, Pfeffer,
50g Fett
4 hartgekochte Eier

Zubereitung

Eischnee schlagen. Das eingeweichte, fest ausgedrückte Brötchen mit Salz, Pfeffer, Zwiebel, Eigelb, Gehacktem u. Eischnee vermengen. Um jedes Ei runde Bällchen formen. In Fett 6-8 Min.

Swallows' Nests (Schwalbennester)

Ingredients:

Metric		Imperial	
250 g	minced beef	1/2 lb	minced beef
250 g	minced pork	1/2 lb	minced pork
1	roll	1	roll
1	egg	1	egg
1	onion	1	onion
	salt, pepper		salt, pepper
50 g	lard or margarine	2 oz	lard or margarine
4	hard boiled eggs	4	hard boiled eggs

Method:

Whisk egg whites until stiff. Soak roll in a little water or milk. Squeeze out excess fluid. Blend with minced meat and stiffly beaten egg whites. Cover each hard boiled egg with meat mixture to form balls. Deep fry in hot lard (or margarine) until brown. Cut in half before serving.

braunbraten. Vor dem Anrich=
ten quer durchschneiden.

Wer es liebt, in Mayonnaise
anrichten.

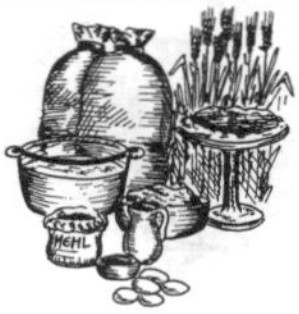
MEHL

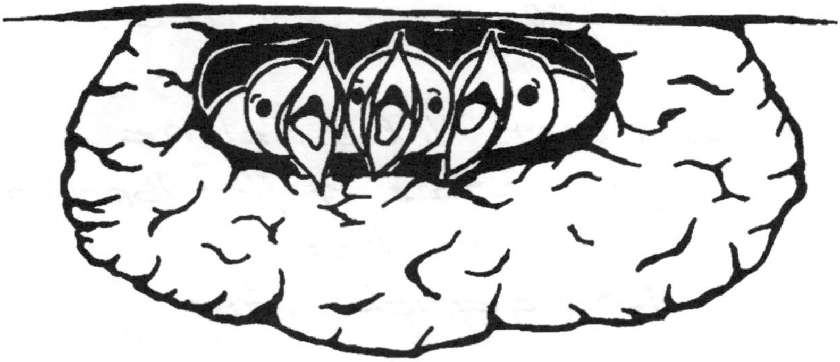

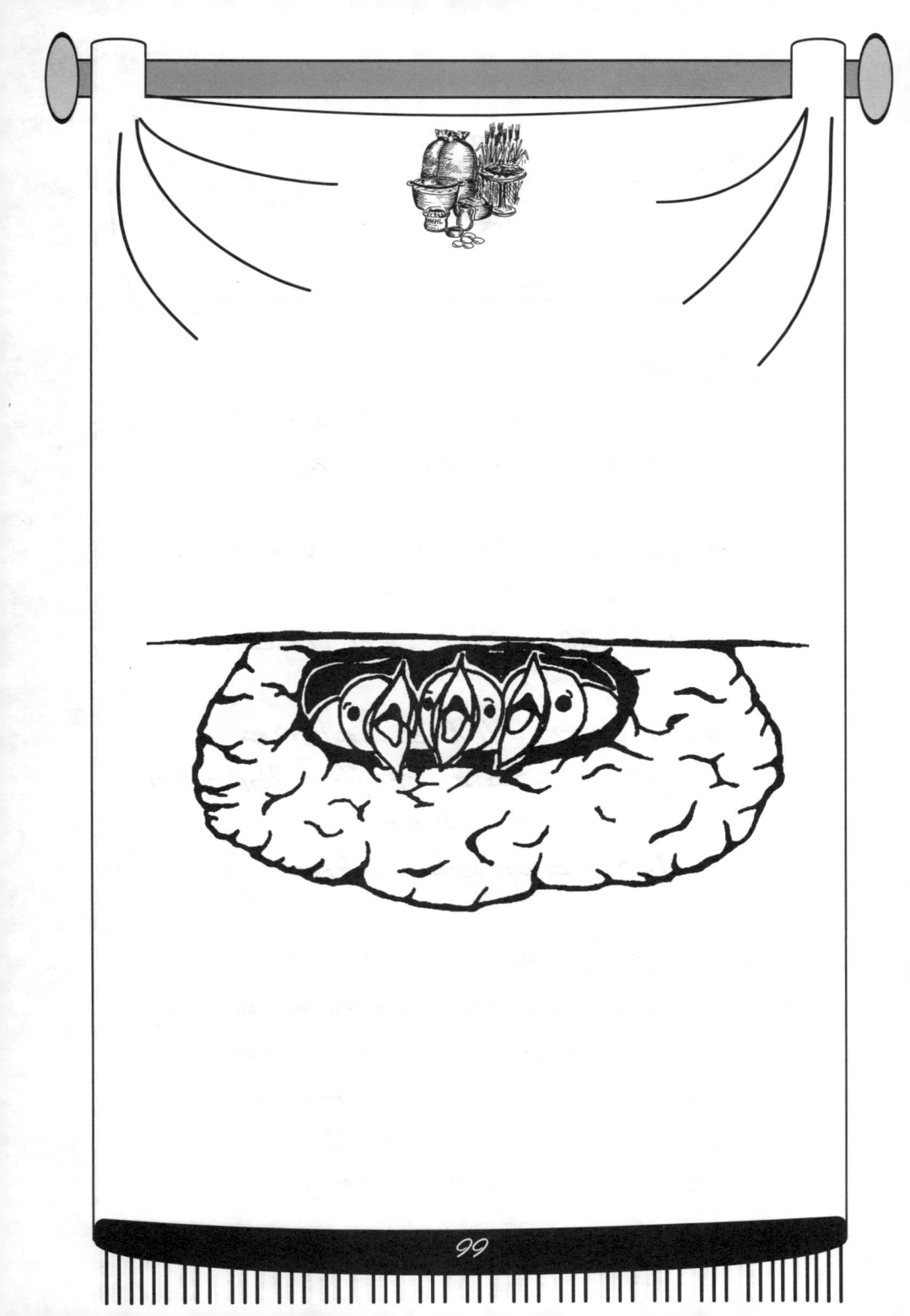

Champignon-Käse-Torte

Zutaten

Teig: 150g Mehl, ½ Teel. Backpulver, 75g Marg., 1 Pr. Salz, 1 Ei

Füllung: 250g Champignons
250g Tomaten
200g gek. Schinken

Guß: 4 Eier, 1/8 l s. Sahne
je 1 Pr. Salz, Pfeffer, Paprika, Muskat
125g gerieb. Käse

Zubereitung

Knetteig bereiten u. kaltstellen, auf den Boden einer Springform ausrollen, einen 3cm hohen Rand andrüken u. im Ofen bei 200-225° 10-15 Minuten vorbacken.

Cheese and Mushroom Pie
(Champignon-Käse-Torte)

Ingredients:

Metric Imperial

Pastry:
150 g	flour	5 oz	flour
1/2 t	baking powder	1/2 t	baking powder
75 g	margarine	3 oz	margarine
1 pinch	salt	1 pinch	salt
1	egg	1	egg

Filling:
250 g	mushrooms	1/2 lb	mushrooms
250 g	tomatoes	1/2 lb	tomatoes
200 g	cooked ham	7 oz	cooked ham

Topping:
4	eggs	4	eggs
125 ml	soured cream	1/4 pint	soured cream
1 pinch	each of salt, pepper, paprika, grated nutmeg	1 pinch	each of salt, pepper, paprika, grated nutmeg

Vorbereitete Champignons ganz dünn schneiden, Tomaten überbrühen, abziehen u. achteln. Schinken würfeln, alles auf den Boden verteilen. Eier mit Sahne, Gewürzen u. Käse verquirlen, über die Masse gießen u. backen.
Bei 180 - 190° 40 - 45 Min.
danach noch 5 - 10 Min. bei 0°.

Tip: Die Torte, kann fertig gebacken, 2-3 Mon. eingefroren gelagert werden. Bei 180-190° etwa 40-45 Min. auftauen und erwärmen.

Method:

For pastry, mix ingredients well to a smooth dough. Chill. Roll out and line bottom and sides of springform tin. Bake in preheated oven at 200-225° C (400-450° F) for 10-15 minutes.

Prepare mushrooms. Slice thinly. Cover tomatoes with boiling water. Leave for 1 minute, then drain, peel and cut each into 8 wedges. Dice ham. Cover pre-baked pastry with above mixture. Whisk eggs with soured cream, add spices and cheese. Pour over mushroom and ham mixture.

Bake at 180-190° C (350-375° F) for 40-45 minutes. Turn off oven and leave pie in oven for another 10-15 minutes.

**He who desires to eat well
should not insult the cook.**
Chinese Proverb

*Wer gut essen will,
darf den Koch nicht beleidigen.*
aus China

Salads

(Salate)

Käsesalat

Zutaten: 350 g Gouda
2 feste Bananen
2 Äpfel
1 Dose Mandarinen
3 Essiggurken

Marinade: 1 Becher Joghurt
5 EßL. Mayonnaise
etwas Salz, Pfeffer, Zucker, Senf
evtl. Essig

Zubereitung:
Marinade zubereiten und abschmekken. Käse in kleine Würfel, Bananen, Gurken und Äpfel in Streifen schneiden und mit der Marinade vermischen.

Cheese Salad (Käsesalat)

Ingredients:

Metric		Imperial	
350 g	mild cheese	14 oz	mild cheese
2	not too soft bananas	2	not too soft bananas
2	apples	2	apples
1 can	mandarins	1 can	mandarins
3	gherkins	3	gherkins

Salad Sauce:

200 ml	yoghurt	8 fl oz	yoghurt
5 T	mayonnaise	5 T	mayonnaise

some salt, pepper, sugar, mustard, vinegar (optional)

Method:

For sauce, mix all ingredients well.

Dice cheese. Peel, core and dice apples. Slice bananas and gherkins into thin strips. Mix all ingredients well with salad sauce.

Käse-Wurst-Salat

Zutaten:
- 125g Fleischwurst oder Mortadella
- 125g Edamer oder Gouda
- 1-2 Äpfel
- 1-2 Gewürzgurken
- 1 Zwiebel
- 100g Mayonnaise oder Essigmarinade
- etwas Senf
- Tomaten

Zubereitung:
Die Zutaten in Würfel schneiden, mit Mayonnaise oder Essigmarinade, mit Senf gewürzt, mischen.

Anrichtevorschlag:
Den Salat in ausgehöhlten Tomaten anrichten.

Cheese and Cold Meat Salad (Käse-Wurst-Salat)

Ingredients:

Metric		Imperial	
125 g	diced cold meat/ pork sausage	5 oz	diced cold meat/ pork sausage
125 g	diced mild cheese	5 oz	diced mild cheese
1-2	apples	1-2	apples
1-2	gherkins	1-2	gherkins
1	onion	1	onion
100 g	mayonnaise or sauce vinaigrette some mustard tomatoes	4 oz	mayonnaise or sauce vinaigrette some mustard tomatoes

Method:

Peel and chop onion. Peel, core and dice apples. Dice meat, cheese and gherkins. Blend mustard into mayonnaise, and add to other ingredients. Serve in scooped out tomato halves.

Käse-Eier-Salat

Zutaten: 200g mittelalter Holländer Käse
2 Essiggurken
4 hartgek. Eier
1 Eßl. Kapern
3 Tomaten
1 Zwiebel
1 Prise Salz
Zitronensaft

Mayonnaise: 1 Eigelb
1 Eßl. Zitronensaft
1 Teel. Senf
Salz
Zucker
1/8 L Öl
etwas Weißwein

Zubereitung:

Käse, Gurken, Eier, Tomaten und Zwiebel in feine Würfel schneiden. Sämtliche Zutaten mit Zitronensaft und Salz vermischen und einige

Egg and Cheese Salad (Käse-Eier-Salat)

Ingredients:

Metric		Imperial	
200 g	medium-strong Dutch cheese	8 oz	medium-strong Dutch cheese
2	gherkins	2	gherkins
4	hard boiled eggs	4	hard boiled eggs
1 T	capers	1 T	capers
3	tomatoes	3	tomatoes
1	onion	1	onion
1 pinch	salt	1 pinch	salt
	lemon juice		lemon juice

Mayonnaise:

1	egg yolk	1	egg yolk
1 T	lemon juice	1 T	lemon juice
1 t	mustard	1 t	mustard
	salt, sugar		salt, sugar
125 ml	salad oil	1/4 pint	salad oil
	some white wine		some white wine

Zeit durchziehen lassen. Das Eigelb verschlagen und mit Zitronensaft, Senf, Salz und Zucker verrühren und das Öl unterschlagen, bis die Mayonnaise dicklich ist. Mit etwas Wein abschmecken und den Salat vorsichtig untermischen.
Salat vor dem Servieren einige Zeit kalt stellen.

Method:

Peel onion. Dice cheese, gherkins, eggs, tomatoes and onion. Season with lemon juice and salt. Leave to marinate for a while. Whisk egg yolk. Blend in lemon juice, mustard, salt and sugar. Gradually add oil, whilst constantly whisking until mayonnaise starts thickening. Season to taste. Carefully blend in some wine. Chill before serving.

Reissalat I

Zutaten:
- 150g gek. Reis
- 1 Dose Thunfisch
- 1 P. Mayonnaise
- 1 Dose Mandarinen
- 2 Teel. Currypulver
- saure Sahne
- Salz

Zubereitung:
Reis mit Thunfisch und Mayonnaise vermischen, Mandarinen vorsichtig unterheben, Curry und saure Sahne (Menge nach Belieben) untermischen, mit Salz abschmekken.

Rice Salad (Reissalat)

Ingredients:

Metric		Imperial	
150 g	boiled rice	6 oz	boiled rice
1 can	tuna fish	1 can	tuna fish
150 g	mayonnaise	6 oz	mayonnaise
1 can	mandarins	1 can	mandarins
2 t	curry powder	2 t	curry powder
	soured cream		soured cream
	salt		salt

Method:

Mix rice, tuna fish and mayonnaise. Carefully stir in mandarines, curry powder and soured cream (as desired). Season to taste.

Herrensalat

Zutaten:
- 500g Rindfleisch
- 500g Tomaten
- 5 Zwiebeln
- 5 gek. Eier
- 1 Salatgurke
- 1 kl. Dose Champignons
- Essig, Öl, Salz, Pfeffer

Zubereitung:

Fleisch kochen und kaltstellen. Tomaten, Salatgurke und Zwiebeln in Scheiben schneiden, Fleisch kleinschneiden und dazugeben, Eier achteln und mit den Champignons unterheben.

Aus Essig, Öl, Salz und Pfeffer eine Marinade bereiten und darübergießen.

Nicht zu früh anrichten, da der Salat sonst zuviel Saft zieht.

Gentlemans Salad (Herrensalat)

Ingredients:

Metric		Imperial	
500 g	beef	1 lb	beef
500 g	tomatoes	1 lb	tomatoes
5	onions	5	onions
5	hardboiled eggs	5	hardboiled eggs
1	cucumber	1	cucumber
1	small can mushrooms	1	small can mushrooms
	vinegar, oil, salt, pepper		vinegar, oil, salt, pepper

Method:
Cook meat until tender and let cool. Peel onions and cucumber. Slice tomatoes, cucumber and onions. Cut meat into small strips and add. Shell eggs and cut into eighths. Add with mushrooms to the other ingredients. Prepare a salad sauce (sauce vinaigrette) out of vinegar, oil, salt and pepper. Pour sauce over the salad shortly before serving. The salad will otherwise draw too much fluid.

Gemüsesalat

Zutaten: 1 kl. Dose Spargel
1 kl. Dose Brechbohnen
1 Glas Erbsen u. Möhren
1 kl. Glas Mais (nach Geschmack)

Zubereitung:
Salatsoße mit saurer Sahne, Salz, Essig und Pfeffer anmachen und das abgetropfte Gemüse unterheben.

Vegetable Salad (Gemüsesalat)

Ingredients:

    1 small can asparagus
    1 small can green beans
    1 jar peas and carrots
    1 small can sweet corn (optional)

Method:

Drain all vegetables well. Prepare a salad sauce out of soured cream, salt, vinegar and pepper. Mix in vegetables.

Hackfleischsalat

Zutaten: 375 g gemischtes Hackfleisch ohne Zwiebel
1 Dose Pilze
1 " Mandarinen
1 " Ananas 320g

Soße: 100g Mayonnaise
1 Teel. Senf
2 Eßl. Mandarinensaft
2 " Tomatenketchup
Salz
Pfeffer
Paprika

Zubereitung:
Hackfleisch in kleine Bällchen formen und braten. Kalt werden lassen und mit den übrigen Zutaten vermischen.

Minced Meat Salad (Hackfleischsalat)

Ingredients:

Metric		Imperial	
375 g	mixed minced meat (beef and pork)	15 oz	mixed minced meat (beaf and pork)
1 can	mushroom	1 can	mushrooms
1 can	mandarins	1 can	mandarins
1 can	pineapple chunks (320 g)	1 can	pineapple chunks (approx. 13 oz)

Sauce:
100 g	mayonnaise	4 oz	mayonnaise
1 t	mustard	1 t	mustard
2 T	ketchup	2 T	ketchup
	salt, pepper, paprika		salt, pepper, paprika

Method:
Season minced meat with salt, pepper and paprika. Form small balls and deep fry until done. Leave to cool, then mix with drained fruit and vegetables. Prepare sauce and add to salad. Chill before serving.

6 - Salat

Zutaten:
- 6 Kartoffeln
- 6 Eier
- 6 saure Gurken
- 6 Äpfel
- 6 Zwiebeln
- 1 Glas Seelachsschnitzel

Marinade:
- 2 Eigelb
- 1 Prise Salz
- " Zucker
- " Pfeffer
- etwas Öl
- " Senf
- " Essig

Zubereitung:

Salz, Zucker und Pfeffer auf das Eigelb geben, verrühren und tropfenweise Öl zugeben, zuletzt Essig und Senf.

Die obigen Zutaten kleinschneiden, in die Marinade geben und umrühren.

6 - Salad (6 - Salat)

Ingredients:

- 6 boiled potatoes
- 6 boiled eggs
- 6 gherkins
- 6 apples
- 6 onions
- 1 jar pickled coal-fish (pollack)

Sauce:

- 2 egg yolks
- 1 pinch salt
- 1 pinch sugar
- 1 pinch pepper
- some oil
- some mustard
- some vinegar

Method:

To prepare salad, dice all ingredients.
For sauce: whisk salt, sugar, pepper and yolks. Gradually add oil in a thin stream. When sauce begins to thicken, carefully whisk in vinegar and mustard. Mix in with salad. Chill before serving.

Heringssalat

Zutaten:
- 2 P. Matjesfilet
- 1 P. Heringssalat
- 1 Apfel
- 2 hartgek. Eier
- 2 Gurken
- Zwiebelringe

Zubereitung:

Matjesfilet, Heringssalat, Apfel, hartgek. Eier und Gurken in Würfel schneiden. Alles verrühren und mit Salz und Pfeffer abschmecken.

Herring Salad (Heringssalat)

Ingredients:

Metric		Imperial	
500 g	pickled herring	1 lb	pickled herring
250 g	ready-to-serve herring salad	1/2 lb	ready-to-serve herring salad
1	apple	1	apple
2	hard-boiled eggs	2	hard-boiled eggs
2	gherkins	2	gherkins
1	medium onion	1	medium onion

Method:

Dice all ingredients. Mix and season with salt and pepper.

Brabanter Salat

Zutaten:
- 2 Stück Chicorée
- 2 " Äpfel (Boskop)
- 1 Eßl. Rosinen
- 1 kl. Dose Mandarinen
- 200 g junger Holland-Gouda
- 1 Becher Joghurt
- 2 Eßl. Honig
- 1/2 Teel. scharfer Senf
- Saft einer Zitrone
- Saft einer halben Apfelsine
- einige Salatblätter

Zubereitung:
Chicorée waschen und in Streifen schneiden. Die Rosinen in warmem Wasser quellen lassen. Äpfel in dünne Scheibchen schneiden. Chicorée und Äpfel mit den gut abgetropften Mandarinen und Rosinen, sowie dem in feine Streifen geschnittenen Gouda mischen.
Die Soße zubereiten und über die Salatzutaten gießen.
Salat vor dem Servieren kurze Zeit kühl stellen.

Salad Brabant Style (Brabanter Salat)

Ingredients:

Metric		Imperial	
2 buds	chicory	2 buds	chicory
2	apples	2	apples
1 T	raisins	1 T	raisins
1 small can mandarins		1 small can mandarins	
200 g	mild Gouda (Dutch cheese)	8 oz	mild Gouda (Dutch cheese)
200 ml	yoghurt	8 fl oz	yoghurt
2 T	honey	2 T	honey
1/2 t	hot mustard	1/2 t	hot mustard
	juice of one lemon		juice of one lemon
	juice of half an orange		juice of half an orange
	some lettuce leaves		some lettuce leaves

Method:

Wash and core chicory. Cut into strips. Soak raisins im luke-warm water. Peel apples and cut into thin slices. Drain mandarins and raisins. Mix with chicory, apples and finely cut cheese. Prepare sauce out of yoghurt, honey, mustard and juices. Pour over salad. Chill before serving.

Geflügelsalat

Zutaten: 1 Huhn (etwa 2½ - 3 kg.)
1 mittlere Sellerieknolle
1 große Möhre
1 Zwiebel
1 Nelke
2 schwarze Pfefferkörner
2 Teel. Salz

Mayonnaise: 1 Eigelb
1 Teel. Salz
½ " Zucker
1 Prise Pfeffer
½ Teel. Paprika
1 Eßl. Zitronensaft
⅛ L Öl
2 Eßl. Weißwein

Zubereitung:

Das Huhn in wenig kochend-heißes Wasser geben, es soll nur eben bedeckt sein. Zwiebel, Nelke, Pfefferkörner sowie Salz von Anfang an dazugeben. Anschließend schwach kochen lassen,

Poultry Salad (Geflügelsalat)

Ingredients:

Metric		Imperial	
1	chicken (2.5-3 kg)	1	chicken (4-6 lbs)
1	medium-sized celeriac	1	medium-sized celeriac
1	large carrot	1	large carrot
1	onion	1	onion
1	clove	1	clove
2 corns	black pepper	2 corns	black pepper
2 t	salt	2 t	salt

Mayonnaise:
1	egg yolk
1 t	salt
1/2 t	sugar
1 pinch	pepper
1/2 t	paprika
1 T	lemon juice
125 ml/5 fl oz	salad oil
2 T	white wine

bis es gar ist. ½ Stunde vor Beendigung der Garzeit Sellerie und Möhre hinzufügen. Das erkaltete, von den Knochen gelöste Fleisch in gleichmäßig feine Streifen, Möhren und Sellerie in Würfel schneiden. Aus den angegebenen Zutaten eine Mayonnaise herstellen, die mit Wein abgeschmeckt und verdünnt wird.
Den Salat mit der Mayonnaise vermischen und kalt stellen.

<u>Veränderung:</u>
Statt mit Möhre und Sellerie kann der Geflügelsalat auch mit Ananas oder Champignons vermischt werden.

Method:

Clean and prepare chicken and put into large casserole. Add boiling water to cover chicken. Add quartered onion, clove, pepper corns and salt. Bring to the boil. Leave to simmer over moderate heat. Before chicken is done, add peeled and roughly sliced carrot and celeriac and let simmer until all ingredients are done. Remove vegetables and chicken from stock and leave to cool. Once cool, separate meat from chicken bones and slice into thin strips. Dice cooked vegetables.

Prepare mayonnaise. Add some wine to round off the taste, then mix in meat and vegetables.

TIP:

Alternatively, the salad may be prepared with pineapple and mushrooms instead of carrots and celeriac.

Möhren-Äpfel-Rohkost

Zutaten: 200 g Möhren
200 g Äpfel

Marinade: 3 Eßl. Öl
2-3 Eßl. Wasser
1-2 Eßl. Zitronensaft
etwas Salz
" Zucker

Zubereitung:
Möhren und Äpfel raffeln und sofort mit der Zitronenmarinade vermischen.

Raw Carrot and Apple Salad
(Möhren-Äpfel-Rohkost)

Ingredients:

Metric		Imperial	
200 g	carrots	8 oz	carrots
200 g	apples	8 oz	apples

Sauce:
- 3 T   salad oil
- 2-3 T   water
- 1-2 T   lemon juice
-    some sugar and salt

Method:
To prepare sauce, mix all sauce ingredients well. Clean and shred carrots and apples; blend in sauce.

Erbsensalat

Zutaten: 250 g gek. Schinken
300 g Tiefkühlerbsen
1 kl. Dose Ananas
1 Dose Champignons
500 g Miracel Whip
Petersilie

Zubereitung:
Schinken, Ananas und Champignons kleinschneiden, Erbsen zugeben und Miracel Whip unterheben. Petersilie überstreuen.

Pea Salad (Erbsensalat)

Ingredients:

Metric		Imperial	
250 g	cooked ham	1/2 lb	cooked ham
300 g	frozen peas	12 oz	frozen peas
1 small can	pineapple bits	1 small can	pineapple bits
1 can	mushrooms	1 can	mushrooms
500 g	salad cream	1 lb	salad cream
	bouquetparsely		bouquetparsley

Method:

Cook peas shortly. Leave to cool. In the meantime, cut ham, pineapple and mushrooms into pieces. Add peas. Stir in salad cream. Serve with chopped parsely scattered over the top.

Rotkohlsalat

Zutaten:
- 1 Dose Rotkohl
- 1 Dose Mandarinen
- 2 Eßl. Mandarinensaft
- 2 rohe geschnittene Paprika
- Salz
- Pfeffer
- Öl
- Essig

Zubereitung:

Alles zusammen vermischen und abschmecken.

Red Cabbage Salad (Rotkohlsalat)

Ingredients:

1 can/jar	red cabbage
1 can	mandarins
2 t	mandarin juice
2	thinly sliced sweet peppers
	salt, pepper, salad oil, vinegar

Method:
Mix all ingredients well. Season to taste.

Many people treat their best table manners as they would their best wear: they would put on both only on festive occasions.

Viele Menschen bekandeln ihre Tischmanieren ähnlich wie ihre guten Kleider: sie nehmen beide nur bei festlichen Gelegenheiten in Gebrauch.

Desserts

(Nachspeisen)

Gebackene Pfirsiche

Zutaten:

- 25 g Zucker
- 1 P. Vanillinzucker
- 1 Ei
- 250 g Mehl
- 1/2 P. Backpulver
- 1/4 L Milch
- Pfirsichhälften

Zubereitung:

Aus den Zutaten einen nicht zu flüssigen Teig bereiten. Pfirsichhälften eintauchen und schwimmend in Kokosfett ausbacken. Noch warm mit Zucker und Zimt bestreut servieren.

Baked Peaches (Gebackene Pfirsiche)

Ingredients:

Metric		Imperial	
25 g	sugar	1 oz	sugar
1/2 t	vanilla extract	1/2 t	vanilla extract
1	egg	1	egg
250 g	flour	1/2 lb	flour
2-3 t	baking powder	2-3 t	baking powder
250 ml	milk	1/2 pint	milk
	peach halves		peach halves

Method:
Drain peaches. Prepare a not too thin batter. Dip each peach half into batter, shake off surplus, then deep fry to a golden crust. Drain well on absorbent paper before serving. Whilst still hot, dust peaches with sugar and cinnamon.

Schusterbuben

Zutaten: (1 Portion)
- ca. 10 reife Zwetschgen
- 1/8 L leichtes, helles Bier
- 125 g Mehl
- 1 Eigelb
- 80 g Zucker
- 1 Teel. Öl
- 1 Prise Salz
- 1 Eiweiß
- Fett z. Ausbacken
- Vanillesoße

Zubereitung:

Zwetschgen waschen, oben sternförmig einschneiden u. Kern entfernen. Alle Zutaten (außer Eiweiß) zu einem dickflüssigen Teig verrühren. Eischnee schlagen und unter den Teig heben. Zwetschgen einzeln in den Teig tauchen und in heißem Fett ausbacken. Sofort mit Vanillesoße servieren.

Cobbler's Laddies (Schusterbuben)

Ingredients (for one portion):

Metric		Imperial	
approx. 10 ripe plums		approx. 10 ripe plums	
125 ml	light beer	1/4 pint	light beer
125 g	plain flour	5 oz	plain flour
1	egg yolk	1	egg yolk
80 g	sugar	3 oz	sugar
1 t	vegetable oil	1 t	vegetable oil
1 pinch	salt	1 pinch	salt
1	egg white	1	egg white
	fat for deep frying		fat for deep frying

Method:

Wash plums, cut top crosswise and stone. Prepare a smooth but not too thin batter by briskly mixing egg yolk, sugar, oil, salt and sifted flour. Fold in stiffly whipped egg white. Dip each plum into batter, shake off surplus, then deep fry to a golden crust. Drain on absorbent paper before serving. Serve with vanilla sauce while still hot.

Gebackene Holunderblüten

Zutaten:
- 3 Eßl. Mehl
- 1 Ei
- ½ Eßl. Öl
- etwas Milch oder Wasser
- schöne Blütendolden des Schwarzen Holunder

Zubereitung:

Ei mit Mehl, Öl und Milch zu einem eben noch flüssigen Teig glatt verrühren. Blütendolden darin gut untertauchen und in reichlich Fett in der Pfanne ausbacken.

Ist der Teig zu dick, wird er an der Innenseite der Dolde nicht gar: dann Stiel abknipsen und Dolde auch von der anderen Seite backen.

Statt Holunder kann man auch die Blüten der Akazie nehmen.

Fried Elder-berry Blossoms
(Gebackene Holunderblüten)

Ingredients:

3 T	plain flour
1	egg
1/2 T	cooking oil
	some milk or water
	elder-berry blossoms

Method:

Place batter ingredients in mixing bowl. Beat well until smooth but not thin. Dip each umbel into batter. Shake lightly to remove surplus. Deep fry to a golden crust and drain well on absorbent paper before serving. If batter is too thick the inside of battered umbel will not fry evenly. Remove the stem of umbel and turn umbel to fry on the other side. Alternatively, acacia blossoms may be used instead of elder-berry.

Quarkschmarren

Zutaten:
- 500 g Quark
- 1/2 l Milch
- 4 Eier
- 150 g Mehl
- 1 P. Vanillinzucker
- 1 Prise Salz
- 200 g Rosinen
- 2 Eßl. Rum
- 100 g Zucker
- Butter od. Marg. z. Backen
- Puderzucker

Zubereitung:

Quark mit Milch glattrühren; Eigelb, Mehl, Vanillinzucker u. Salz zugeben. Rosinen waschen, mit Rum beträufeln u. beifügen. Eiweiß zu Schnee schlagen, den Zucker nach u. nach einrieseln lassen, vorsichtig unter den Quark ziehen. In einer großen Pfanne Fett zerlassen, etwas Quarkmasse hineingeben und

Curd Broken Pancake (Quarkschmarren)

Ingredients:

Metric		Imperial	
500 g	curd	1 lb	curd
500 ml	milk	1 pint	milk
4	eggs (separated)	4	eggs (separated)
150 g	plain flour	6 oz	plain flour
1/2 t	vanilla essence	1/2 t	vanilla essence
1 pinch	salt	1 pinch	salt
200g	seedless raisins	8 oz	seedless raisins
2 T	rum	2 T	rum
100 g	sugar	4 oz	sugar
	lard or oil for frying		lard or oil for frying
	icing sugar		icing sugar

Method:

Soak raisins in rum. Place curd and milk in large bowl. Whisk until creamy. Blend in egg yolks, sifted flour, vanilla and salt. Add raisins. Beat egg whites until stiff, gradually adding sugar. Fold into curd mixture.

glattstreichen, den Pfannekuchen von beiden Seiten goldgelb braten, dann mit Gabeln in Stücke zerreißen, auf einer Platte warmstellen. Mit dem restlichen Teig ebenso verfahren.
Die Schmarren mit Puderzucker bestreuen und mit Apfelmus oder mit Nelken gewürztem Apfelkompott servieren.

Heat some fat in frying pan. Pour in a small portion of curd mixture into pan to thickly coat base. Cook on both sides to a golden brown. Using two forks, tear pancake into small pieces. Turn out onto platter and keep warm. Repeat procedure until batter has been used up. When all pancakes are done, sprinkle with icing sugar. Serve with apple sauce or apple compôte.

Herrencreme

Zutaten:

- 1 P. Puddingpulver
- 1/2 l Milch
- 2 Eßl. (schwach gehäuft) Zucker
- 1/8 l Sahne
- 50 g zartbittere Schokolade
- Rum n. Geschmack

Zubereitung:

Puddingpulver u. Zucker mit 6 Eßl. Milch anrühren. Die Milch (1/2 L) zum Kochen bringen, von der Platte nehmen und angerührtes Puddingpulver einrühren, kurz aufkochen lassen. Erkalten lassen. Geschlagene Sahne, grob geraspelte Schokolade und den Rum vorsichtig unter den Pudding heben.

Gentlemans Cream Pudding (Herrencreme)

Ingredients:

Metric		Imperial	
50 g	custard powder	2 oz	custard powder
500 ml	milk	1 pint	milk
2 level T	sugar	2 level T	sugar
125 ml	single cream	1/4 pint	single cream
50 g	plain chocolate	2-3 oz	plain chocolate
	some rum		some rum

Method:

Mix custard powder, sugar and 6 T milk to a paste. Bring rest of milk to the boil. Remove saucepan from heat and whisk in custard paste. Boil once more. Remove from heat and leave to cool. Stir in coursely grated chocolate, stiffly beaten single cream and some rum. Chill before serving.

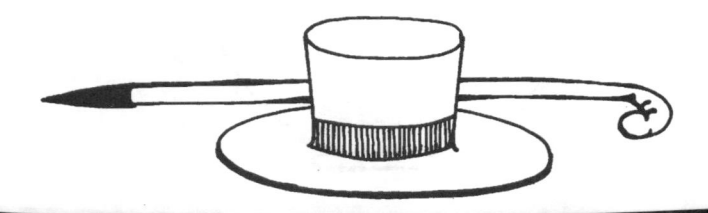

Preiselbeerpudding

Zutaten: 1 Tasse Preiselbeeren
           1/2 Pfd. Zucker
           3   Eiweiß

Zubereitung:

Die Zutaten eine halbe Stunde nach einer Seite rühren. Dazu eine Vanillesoße reichen.

(Aus einem Kochkurs um 1910)

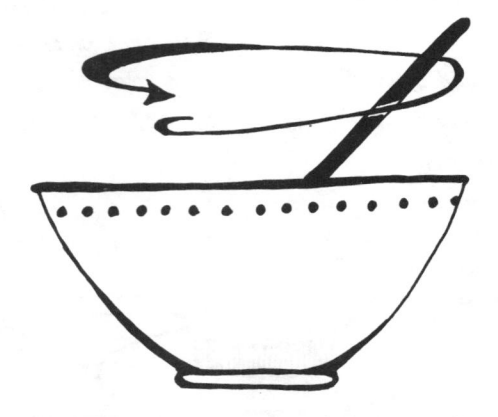

Cranberry Pudding (Preiselbeerpudding)

Ingredients:
1 cup	cranberries
250 g/1/2 lb	sugar
3	egg whites

Method:
Put all ingredients in bowl and stir constantly in one direction for about 30 min. Serve with vanilla sauce.

(This recipe originated in a cookery class in 1910)

Grapefruit - Sahnecreme

Zutaten:
- 4 Eigelb
- 100 g Zucker
- 4 Eßl. frischgepr. Grapefruitsaft
- 1 Eßl. Zitronensaft
- 4 Blatt weiße Gelatine
- 4 Eiweiß
- 1/8 l Sahne

Zubereitung:

Eigelb u. Zucker schaumig rühren, den Grapefruit- u. Zitronensaft dazugeben. Die kalt eingeweichte Gelatine ausdrücken, auflösen, zur Schaummasse geben u. unterrühren. Sobald sie anfängt zu gelieren, Eischnee und geschlagene Sahne unterheben, in Schälchen füllen und mit einigen Sahnetupfern garnieren.

Grapefruit Créme (Grapefruit - Sahnecreme)

Ingredients:

Metric		Imperial	
4	egg yolks	4	egg yolks
100 g	sugar	4 oz	sugar
4 T	fresh grapefruit juice	4 T	fresh grapefruit juice
1 T	lemon juice	1 T	lemon juice
2 t	gelatine	2 t	gelatine
4	egg whites	4	egg whites
125 ml	single cream	1/4 pint	single cream

Method:

Beat egg yolks and sugar until thick and creamy. Add grapefruit and lemon juice. Mix gelatine and 1 T of water in a small bowl. Place bowl in a pan of water over moderate heat. Stir until gelatine has dissolved. Leave gelatine paste to cool but not to set. Once cool, add gelatine to egg mixture. When mixture starts thickening, fold in stiffly beaten egg whites and stiffly whipped cream. Serve with whipped cream.

Hexencreme

Zutaten: 4 große Äpfel
1 Eiweiß
etwas Zitronensaft
oder Wein
etwas Zitronenschale
etwas Zucker

Zubereitung:

Die Äpfel werden gebraten und zu Brei gerührt. Eiweiß mit Zitronensaft, Zucker und Zitronenschale etwa 15 Min. schlagen und unter die Äpfel rühren.

Witchs Créme (Hexencreme)

Ingredients:

4	large apples
1	egg white
	some lemon juice or wine
	some grated rind of an untreated lemon
	some sugar

Method:

Fry peeled, cored and sliced apple, then stir to a pulp. Whisk egg whites with lemon juice, lemon rind and sugar for approx. 15 min. Blend into apple pulp.

Rosa Samtspeise

Zutaten: 1/4 l Saft
5 Blatt rote Gelatine
1/4 l sauren Rahm
Zucker n. Geschmack

Zubereitung:

Die Gelatine einweichen und warm auflösen, mit Fruchtsaft vermischen. Die Sahne mit dem Zucker schaumig schlagen und in den Fruchtsaft geben. Die Speise 10-15 Min. gut rühren bis alles steif ist.

Red Velvet Cream (Rosa Samtspeise)

Ingredients:

Metric		Imperial	
250 ml	fruit juice	1/2 pint	fruit juice
2 t	red jello	2 t	red jello
1 T	water	1 T	water
250 ml	soured cream	1/2 pint	soured cream
	sugar		sugar

Method:

Measure 1 T water into a small basin and add jello powder. Place basin in a pan of water over moderate heat an stir until jello has dissolved. Leave to cool but not to set. Mix well with fruit juice.
Whisk soured cream with sugar until creamy. Add to jello and whisk for another 10-15 min.

Eiergelee

Zutaten: 1 1/8 L Milch
4 Eier (Eischnee)
5 Eigelb
abgerieb. Schale von 1
 Zitrone
Zucker
etwas Zimt

Zubereitung:

Alle Zutaten in einer tiefen Schüssel verrühren. Schüssel abdecken und in kochendes Wasser stellen bis die Eier stocken. Gelee erkalten lassen und mit Zucker und Zimt bestreuen. Man reicht eingemachte Preiselbeeren dazu.

Egg Jelly (Eiergelee)

Ingredients:

Metric		Imperial	
1 1/8 l	milk	2 1/2 pints	milk
4	eggs whites	4	egg whites
5	egg yolks	5	egg yolks
grated rind of 1 untreated lemon		grated rind of 1 untreated lemon	
	sugar		sugar
	pinch of cinnamon		pinch of cinnamon

Method:

Put all ingredients into a deep fireproof bowl and whisk until creamy. Fold in stiffly beaten egg whites. Cover bowl and place in pan with boiling water over low heat. Leave to set. Chill and sprinkle with sugar and cinnamon. Serve with cranberries.

Obstsalat in Weingelee

Zutaten:

- 1/4 L Weißwein
- 50 g Zucker
- 6 Blatt weiße Gelatine
- 2 " rote Gelatine
- 1 kg Obst (n. Jahreszeit)
- Zitronensaft, Kirschwasser oder Weinbrand
- 1/4 L Schlagsahne

Zubereitung:

Gelatine kalt einweichen u. quellen lassen. Früchte waschen, schälen, kleinschneiden, mit Zucker mischen und mit Alkohol abschmecken. Gelatine aus dem Wasser nehmen u. in einen Kochtopf geben, bei geringer Hitze auflösen und unter den Wein rühren. Obst in eine Schüssel füllen, mit Gelatine verrührten Wein unterheben. Erstarren lassen, auf eine Platte stürzen, mit steifer Schlagsahne verzieren.

Fruit Salad in Wine Jelly
(Obstsalat in Weingelee)

Ingredients:

Metric		Imperial	
250 ml	white wine	1/2 pint	white wine
50 g	sugar	2 oz	sugar
2 t	gelatine	2 t	gelatine
1/2 t	red jello	1/2 t	red jello
1 kg	fruit of the season	2 lb	fruit of the season
	lemon juice		lemon juice
	kirsch or cognac		kirsch or cognac
250 ml	single cream	1/2 pint	single cream

Method:
Measure 1-2 T water into a small basin and add jello and gelatine. Place dish in a pan of water over moderate heat and stir until gelatine and jello have dissolved. Leave to cool, but do not allow to set. Blend in wine. Wash, peel (if necessary) and cut fruit into small pieces. Mix with sugar and round off the taste with some kirsch or cognac. Add to wine jello. Chill and turn out onto serving platter. Serve with whipped cream.

Gefüllte Eis-Äpfel

Zutaten: 4 mittlere Äpfel (Golden Delicious)
1/8 l Wasser
1/4 l Weißwein
Saft einer halben Zitrone
2 Eßl. Zucker
2-3 Eßl. rote Marmelade od. Gelee
1 Familienpackung Fürst-Pückler-Eiscreme

Zubereitung:

Äpfel schälen, einen Deckel abschneiden u. das Innere aushöhlen. Wasser, Wein, Zitronensaft u. Zucker aufkochen, Äpfel 5 Min. darin ziehen lassen u. mit dem Sirup erkalten lassen. Äpfel abtropfen, auf Glasteller stellen u. in den Kühlschrank stellen. Sirup mit Marmelade mischen, mit Rum oder Orangenlikör abschmecken. Äpfel mit Eiscreme füllen, mit der roten Soße umgießen und sofort servieren.

Ice-Cream Apples (Gefüllte Eis-Äpfel)

Ingredients:

Metric		Imperial	
4	medium-sized apples	4	medium-sized apple
125 ml	water	1/4 pint	water
250 ml	white wine	1/2 pint	white wine
	juice of 1 lemon		juice of 1 lemon
2 T	sugar	2 T	sugar
2-3 T	red jam or jelly	2-3 T	red jam or jelly
	ice-cream		ice-cream
	rum or orange liqueur		rum or orange liqueur

Method:

Peel apple and cut off the tops. Hollow out apples. Bring water, wine, juice of half lemon and sugar to the boil. Put in apples and simmer over low heat for about 5 minutes. Leave to cool. Drain apples and place on four dessert plates and chill. Mix cold syrup with jam or jelly. Round off the taste with rum or orange liqueur. Fill apples with ice-cream. Pour red sauce around apples and serve immediately.

Aprikosen „Negus"

Zutaten:
- 1 kl. Dose Aprikosen
- 1 Eßl. Zucker
- 1 P. Vanillinzucker
- 1 Likörglas Apricot-Brandy
- 1 P. (250g) Vanille-Schoko-Eiscreme
- 1/4 L Schlagsahne

Zubereitung:

Aprikosen mit dem Saft, Zucker u. Vanillinzucker aufkochen u. erkalten lassen. Apricot-Brandy daruntergeben. Sahne steifschlagen. Von der Eiscreme mit einem in heißes Wasser getauchten Eßlöffel Späne abschaben, in Gläser verteilen, mit Aprikosen belegen und mit der Sahne garnieren.

Apricot "Negus" (Aprikosen "Negus")

Ingredients:

Metric	Imperial
1 small can apricot halves	1 small can apricot halves
1 T sugar	1 T sugar
1/2 t vanilla extract	1/2 t vanilla extract
1 liqueur glass apricot brandy	1 liqueur glass apricot brandy
250 g vanilla-chocolate ice-cream	1/2 lb vanilla-chocolate ice-cream
250 ml single cream	8 fl oz single cream

Method:

Bring apricots, juice, sugar and vanilla to the boil. Remove from heat. Blend in apricot brandy. Whip cream until stiff. Flake ice-cream into dessert glasses. Put apricots on top of ice-cream and serve with whipped cream.

Omelett mit Rum

Zutaten:
- 5-6 Eier
- 2-3 Eßl. Milch
- 1 Prise Salz
- 1 Eßl. Butter od. Marg.
- 3-4 Eßl. Aprikosenmarmelade
- 2 Eßl. Rum
- 2 Eßl. Zucker
- 2-3 Scheiben Ananas

Zubereitung:

Eier mit Milch und Salz verquirlen. Fett in der Pfanne erhitzen, Eimasse hineingeben u. mit der Gabel rühren, dabei Pfanne schütteln. Die leicht gestockte Eimasse oval zusammenschieben. Rum mit Aprikosenmarmelade verrühren und in die Mitte des Omletts geben. Ränder darüberschlagen, auf eine heiße Platte stürzen u. mit Zucker bestreuen. Rum in eine kl. Schöpfkelle geben, anzünden und darübergießen. Mit Ananas umlegen, sofort servieren.

Rum Omelette (Omelette mit Rum)

Ingredients:

5-6	eggs
2-4 T	milk
1 pinch	salt
1 T	butter or margarine
3-4 T	apricot jam
2 T	rum
2 T	sugar
2-3 slices	pineapple

Method:

Whisk milk, eggs and salt well. Heat fat in pan, pour in egg mixture. Cook slowly until underside is golden and centre is set. Mix rum and jam and pour over the centre of the omelette. Fold over the sides. Turn out onto platter and sprinkle with sugar. Put some rum into ladle set alight and pour over omelette. Garnish with pineapple and serve immediately.

Schokoladen-Pfannkuchen

Zutaten:

- **Teig:**
  - 250 g Mehl
  - 1 Prise Salz
  - 3/8 L Wasser
  - 3 Eier
  - 2 Eßl. Butter od. Margarine
- **Füllung:**
  - 1/2 L Milch
  - 50 g Butter od. Margarine
  - 4 Eßl. (gehäuft) Kaba
  - 2 " " Zucker
  - 1 Prise Salz
  - 2 Eigelb
  - 2 Eßl. (gehäuft) Speisestärke
- **Soße:**
  - 1/2 L Milch
  - 1 P. Vanillinzucker
  - 1 Eßl. Zucker
  - 2 Eiweiß
  - 1 P. Vanillesoße

Zubereitung:

Mehl, Salz und Wasser zu einem Pfannkuchenteig rühren und Pfannkuchen daraus backen, abkühlen lassen. Füllung bereiten: dazu Milch aufkochen, Butter, Kaba, Zucker und Salz gut unterrühren. Eigelb mit der Stärke

Chocolate Pancakes (Schokoladen-Pfannkuchen)

Ingredients:

Metric		Imperial	
Batter:			
250 g	plain flour	1/2 lb	plain flour
	pinch of salt		pinch of salt
375 ml	water	3/4 pint	water
3	eggs	3	eggs
2 T	butter or margarine (melted and cooled)	2 T	butter or margarine (melted and cooled)
Filling:			
500 ml	milk	1 pint	milk
50 g	butter or margarine	2 oz	butter or margarine
4 T	cocoa	4 T	cocoa
2 T	sugar	2 T	sugar
	pinch of salt		pinch of salt
2	egg yolks	2	egg yolks
2 heaped T	corn starch	2 heaped T	corn starch
Sauce:			
500 ml	milk	1 pint	milk
1/2 t	vanilla extract	1/2 t	vanilla extract
1 T	sugar	1 T	sugar
2	egg whites	2	egg whites
25 g	custard powder	1 oz	custard powder

und 1/3 Tasse Milch verrühren. Die erhitzte Milch damit binden. Creme noch heiß auf die Pfannkuchen streichen, abkühlen lassen und zu Rouladen zusammenrollen, in etwa 5-6 cm lange Stücke schneiden und in eine gefettete Auflaufform stellen. Aus den angegebenen Zutaten eine Vanillesoße bereiten, steifen Eischnee unterheben. Rouladen mit Vanillesoße umgießen und im Backofen bei 175° etwa 25 Min. backen.

Method:

Put batter ingredients in a bowl and beat well to give a smooth consistency. Fry pancakes. Leave pancakes to cool.

For the filling, scald the milk, blend in butter, cocoa, sugar and salt. Mix egg yolk, starch and 1/3 cup milk to make a paste, and stir into heated milk until mixture thickens.

Spread the filling over the pancakes. Leave to cool, then roll pancakes and cut them into 5-6 cm (2 inch) pieces. Put pieces upright in a fireproof pie dish.

For the sauce, mix custard powder, 6 T of milk, vanilla and sugar to a paste. Bring milk to the boil. Remove from heat and blend in custard paste. Once cool, fold in stiffly beaten egg whites.

Pour sauce around pancake rolls, and bake in a preheated oven at 175° C (350° F) for about 25 minutes.

Coffee has to be as hot as hell,
as black as the devil,
as pure as an angel
and as sweet as love.
C. M. de Talleyrand

*Der Kaffee muß heiß sein wie die Hölle,
schwarz wie der Teufel,
rein wie ein Engel
und süß wie die Liebe.*
C.M. de Talleyrand

Cakes, Pies and Pastries

(Torten, Kuchen und Gebäck)

Jägertorte

Zutaten:
- 50 g Mehl
- 2 Teel. Backpulver
- 50 g Zucker
- 100 g Margarine
- 1 Eßl. Pulverkaffee
- 4 Eier
- 100 g ger. Nüsse

Zum Bestreichen:
- 1 Eigelb
- 2 Eßl. Zucker
- 1 Eßl. Rum
- 1 Gl. Preiselbeeren 200 g.
- 250 g Sahne
- 1 P. Vanillezucker
- 1 P. Sahnefestiger
- 3-4 Eßl. Eierlikör
- Mokkabohnen

Zubereitung:
Rührteig bereiten, in einer nur am Boden gefetteten Springform glattstreichen und backen.

Hunters Cake (Jägertorte)

Ingredients:

Metric		Imperial	
To make cake:			
50 g	plain flour	2 oz	plain flour
2 t	baking powder	2 t	baking powder
50 g	sugar	2 oz	sugar
100 g	margarine	4 oz	margarine
1 T	instant coffee	1 T	instant coffee
4	eggs	4	eggs
100 g	grated nuts	4 oz	grated nuts
To make topping:			
1	egg yolk	1	egg yolk
2 T	sugar	2 T	sugar
1 T	rum	1 T	rum
200 g	cranberries	8 oz	cranberries
250 ml	single cream	8 fl oz	single cream
1/2 t	vanilla extract	1/2 t	vanilla extract
3-4 T	liqueur egg-flip	3-4 T	liqueur egg-flip
plain chocolate beans/chips		plain chocolate beans/chips	

20-25 Min. bei 180-190°, 5 Min. O.
Nach dem Backen mit einem Messer
die Torte vom Formrand lösen,
auf ein Kuchengitter stürzen und
auskühlen lassen. Das mit Zucker
und Rum verrührte Eigelb daraufstreichen, dann die Preiselbeeren,
danach die mit Vanillezucker und
Sahnefestiger steifgeschlagene Sahne
darübergeben.
Zum Schluß mit Eierlikör bestreichen und mit Mokkabohnen
verzieren.
Die Torte schmeckt am besten,
wenn sie gekühlt serviert wird.

Method:

Whisk margarine, sugar and eggs until light and creamy. Blend in sifted flour and baking powder. Continue beating. Add instant coffee granules and grated nuts. Pour into greased and floured 20 cm (8 inch) spring-form baking tin, and bake in a preheated oven at 180-190° C (350-375° F) for 20-25 minutes or until skewer, inserted into the centre of the cake, comes out clean. Turn off heat and leave cake in oven for another five minutes. Turn out on to a rack to cool.

For topping: Beat egg yolk with rum and sugar; spread over top of cake. Cover with cranberries and dust with vanilla sugar, then spread over stiffly beaten cream. Finally, trickle liqueur egg-flip over cream and garnish with chocolate beans or chocolate chips. Serve chilled.

Schmant-Torte mit Preiselbeeren

Zutaten: 1 Bisquitboden (Wiener)

Füllung:
- 3 B. Bauernschmant
- 3 P. Vanillezucker
- 1 Gl. Preiselbeeren

Belag:
- 1 B. Schlagsahne
- 1 Teel. Zucker
- Schokoladenblättchen oder Streusel

Zubereitung:

3 Becher Bauernschmant mit 3 P. Vanillezucker steifschlagen, die Preiselbeeren unterheben.
Die Torte 2x durchschneiden, mit Preiselbeerschmant füllen. Becher Sahne schlagen, die Torte bestreichen mit Schokoladen-Blättchen oder Streusel bestreuen und mit Sahnetupfern verzieren.

Cranberry Cake
(Schmand-Torte mit Preiselbeeren)

Ingredients:

Metric		Imperial	

Bake a sponge cake as usual in two well-greased and floured sandwich tins. Allow layers to cool.

Filling:
600 ml	double cream	1 pint	double cream
1 1/2 t	vanilla extract or essence	1 1/2 t	vanilla extract or essence
	some sugar		some sugar
	cranberries (compôte)		cranberries (compôte)

Topping:
250 ml	single cream	8 fl oz	single cream
1 t	sugar	1 t	sugar
	chocolate chips		chocolate chips

Method:

Whisk filling ingredients to a stiff consistency. Fold in cranberries. Spread filling over bottom cake layer and sandwich layers together.

Whip single cream and sugar. Spread cake with cream and sprinkle over chocolate chips.

Schmantkuchen

Zutaten:
- 250 g Butter oder Margarine
- 250 g Zucker
- 5 Eier
- 1 P. Vanillezucker
- 250 g Mehl
- 1 P. Backpulver
- 3 B. Bauernschmant
- Kakao

Zubereitung:
Butter, Zucker, Eier und Vanillezucker schaumig rühren. Mit den restlichen Zutaten, Mehl und Backpulver, einen Teig herstellen. 2 Torten backen. Eine helle und eine dunkle mit Kakao. Jede Torte wird nach dem Erkalten halbiert, so daß 4 Böden entstehen. Diese Böden werden nun mit insgesamt 3 Bechern Bauernschmant (im Wechsel mit hellem und dunklem Boden) gefüllt. Oberste Schicht mit Zimt-Zuckerguß bestreichen.

Double Cream Cake (Schmandkuchen)

Ingredients:

Metric		Imperial	
250 g	butter or margarine	1/2 lb	butter or margarine
250 g	sugar	1/2 lb	sugar
5	eggs	5	eggs
1/2 t	vanilla extract or essence	1/2 t	vanilla extract or essence
250 g	plain flour	1/2 lb	plain flour
2 t	baking powder	2 t	baking powder
600 g	double cream	1 1/4 pints	double cream
	cocoa		cocoa

Method:

Put butter, sugar, eggs and vanilla in a deep bowl and whisk briskly to a thick cream. Gradually blend in sifted flour and baking powder. Halve the cake mixture and blend cocoa into one half. Bake two 18 cm (7 inch) cakes, one light and the other dark, at 180° C (350° F) for about 40 minutes or until a skewer, inserted into centre of cake, comes out clean. Turn out onto rack to cook.

Cut each cake in half horizontally. Spread each layer with double cream. Place the layers on each other, alternating light and dark layers. Place the final layer on top and coat cake with a cinnamon glaze.

Birnentorte

Zutaten:

- 5 mittelgr. Birnen
- 1/8 l Weißwein
- 1 Teel. Zimt
- 150 g Butter o. Margar.
- 150 g Zucker
- 3 Eier
- 300 g Mehl
- 1 P. Backpulver
- 6 Eßl. Milch
- 1 geh. Eßl. Kakao
- 4 geh. Eßl. Haferflocken (zart)
- 4 Eßl. Rum
- 1 Messersp. Muskat
- 100 g Halbbitter-Schokolade
- etwas Fett
- 2 Eßl. Puderzucker

Zubereitung:

Halbe Birnen in Wein erhitzen, 1/2 Teel. Zimt dazu, in geschlossener Pfanne 5 Min. garen. Birnen abtropfen lassen. Fett und Zucker

Pear Cake (Birnentorte)

Ingredients:

Metric		Imperial	
5	medium-sized pears peeled, halved, cored	5	medium-sized pears peeled, halved, cored
125 ml	white wine	1/4 pint	white wine
1 t	ground cinnamon	1 t	ground cinnamon
150 g	butter or margarine	6 oz	butter or margarine
150 g	sugar	6 oz	sugar
3	eggs	3	eggs
300 g	plain flour	11 oz	plain flour
2 t	baking powder	2 t	baking powder
6 T	milk	6 T	milk
1 heaped T	cocoa	1 heaped T	cocoa
4 heaped T	oats	4 heaped T	oats
4 T	rum	4 T	rum
1 pinch	ground nutmeg	1 pinch	ground nutmeg
1/2 t	cinnamon	1/2 t	cinnamon
2 T	powder sugar	2 T	powder sugar

Method:

Arrange pear halves in a pan, cored surface facing upwards. Sprinkle over cinnamon.

schaumig rühren, mit Eiern, Mehl, Backpulver, Milch, Kakao, Haferfl., Rum und 1/2 Teel. Zimt vermischen. 2/3 des Teiges in eine Springform geben, glattstreichen. Birnen mit Wölbung nach oben auf den Teig legen. Restlichen Teig darauf verteilen.
60 Min. bei 200° backen.
Mit Puderzucker bestreuen.

Hick

Pour in white wine to cover, bring to the boil, and cook, covered, for about 5 minutes. Drain.

Whisk butter or margarine and sugar until creamy. Add eggs and continue whisking. Blend in sifted flour, baking powder, cocoa, nutmeg, cinnamon and oats, gradually pouring in milk and rum. Grease and flour an 18 cm (7 inch) spring-form baking tin. Pour in 2/3 of cake mixture and spread evenly. Arrange pear halves on top of batter, core surface facing downwards. Pour over the rest of batter. Bake in a preheated oven at 200° C (400° F) for about 60 minutes. Turn out onto rack to cool. Dust with powder sugar.

Hick

Kiwi - Torte

Zutaten:

2		Eier
10	g	Puderzucker
50	g	Zucker
1	P.	Vanillezucker
35	g	Mehl
40	g	Mondamin
1/4	Tl.	Backpulver
200	g	Philadelphia-Käse
250	g	Sahnequark
3	EBl.	Zitronensaft
8	EBl.	Zucker
1	P.	Götterspeise Waldmeister
1	P.	Gelatine
2	B.	Sahne

Zubereitung:

Eigelb mit 2 EBl. heißem Wasser schaumig rühren, Zucker und Vanillezucker unterrühren,

Kiwi Cake (Kiwi-Torte)

Ingredients:

Metric		Imperial	
2	eggs	2	eggs
10 g	icing sugar	1/2 oz	icing sugar
50 g	granulated sugar	2 oz	granulated sugar
1/2 t	vanilla extract or essence	1/2 t	vanilla extract or essence
35 g	plain flour	1 1/4 oz	plain flour
40 g	corn starch	1 1/2 oz	corn starch
1/4 t	baking powder	1/4 t	baking powder
200 g	Philadelphia cream cheese	8 oz	Philadelphia cream cheese
250 g	high fat curd	10 oz	high fat curd
3 T	lemon juice	3 T	lemon juice
8 T	sugar	8 T	sugar
1 pkg	woodruff jello	1 pkg	woodruff jello
1 pkg	gelatine	1 pkg	gelatine
500 ml	whipping cream	1 pint	whipping cream
3-4	ripe/firm kiwis	3-4	ripe/firm kiwis

Method:

Cream egg yolks, 2 T boiling water, sugar and vanilla. Beat egg whites with icing sugar until they form very stiff peaks.

Eiweiß mit Puderzucker steif schlagen und vorsichtig auf die Eigelbmasse legen. Dann Mehl, Mondamin und Backpulver auf die Masse sieben und vorsichtig unter die Masse rühren.
Bei 200-220° ca. 15 Min. hellbraun backen.

Dann den Philadelphiakäse, Sahnequark, Zitronensaft, Zucker, Götterspeise (Pulver) verrühren und die aufgelöste Gelatine unterheben. 2 Becher süße Sahne schlagen mit Vanillezucker ebenfalls unter die Masse rühren und auf dem erkaltetem Boden verteilen und kalt stellen.

3 geschälte und in Scheiben geschnittene Kiwi auflegen.

Aus klarem Tortenguß (mit etwas Zitronensaft und Wasser angerührt) einen Guß zubereiten und über die Kiwitorte geben. Danach wieder kalt stellen.

Spread over egg yolk mixture. Sift flour, corn starch and baking powder over egg white and carefully blend. Pour into greased and floured 20 cm (8 inch) springform baking tin. Bake in a preheated oven at 200°-220° C (400°- 440° F) for approx. 15 minutes. Turn out onto rack and leave to cool.

Whisk cream cheese, curd, lemon juice, 8 T sugar and granulated woodruff jello. Blend in dissolved gelatine. Whip cream with some sugar and vanilla extract and blend into cream cheese mixture. Spread over top of cake base and chill. Peel and slice kiwis and arrange slices on top of cake. Make a clear gelatine glaze (add some sugar and lemon juice). Pour over cake and re-chill.

Käse-Sahne mit Himbeer

Zutaten:
- 125 g Butter
- 125 g Zucker
- 3 Eier
- 100 g Mehl
- 100 g Mondamin
- 1 P. Vanillezucker
- 1 Teel. Backpulver
- etwas Zitrone

Belag:
- 2 Doppelp. Buko (200 g)
- ½ Tasse Puderzucker
- 2 Becher süße Sahne
- Himbeeren

Zutaten:

Die obigen Teigzutaten gut verrühren und in einer Springform eine ½ Stunde backen.
Den Buko gut verrühren; dann den Puderzucker zugeben. Dann die geschlagene Sahne unterheben. Die Himbeeren auf die Käsemasse geben, den Saft andicken und über die Torte laufen lassen.

Cream Cheese Raspberry Cake (Käse - Sahne mit Himbeer)

Ingredients:

Metric		Imperial	

Cake base:

Metric		Imperial	
125 g	butter	5 oz	butter
125 g	sugar	5 oz	sugar
3	eggs	3	eggs
100 g	plain flour	4 oz	plain flour
100 g	corn starch	4 oz	corn starch
1 t	vanilla extract or essence	1 t	vanilla extract of essence
1 t	baking powder	1 t	baking powder
	some lemon juice		some lemon juice

Topping:

Metric		Imperial	
200 g	Philadelphia cream cheese	8 oz	Philadelphia cream cheese
125 g	castor sugar	5 oz	castor sugar
500 ml	whipping cream	1 pint	whipping cream

Method:

To make base:

Cream butter, sugar and eggs. Blend in sifted flour, corn starch, vanilla and baking powder. Add some lemon juice. Pour into well-greased and floured 20 cm (8 inch) spring-form baking tin. Bake in preheated oven at 200° C (400° F) for approx. 30 minutes or until a skewer, inserted into centre of cake, comes out clean. Turn out onto rack and let cool.

To make topping:

Whip cream with castor sugar and blend into whipped cream cheese. Spread over top of cake base. Arrange raspberries on top of cream cheese mixture.

Dissolve some gelatine in raspberry juice. When cool yet still fluid, pour over top of cake. Chill cake before serving.

Herrentorte

Zutaten:
- 200 g gem. Nüsse
- 100 g Zucker
- 4 Eigelb
- 125 g Margarine
- 2 Tl. Backpulver
- 1 Fl. Bittermandel
- 2 Eßl. Kakao

Belag:
- 1 kl. Gl. Preiselbeeren
- 1/4 l Schlagsahne

Zubereitung:

Den Zucker, die 4 Eigelb und die Margarine verrühren. 2 Eßl. Kakao unterrühren. Anschließend die Nüsse, das Backpulver und das Bittermandelöl dazugeben. Danach Eischnee unterziehen.
Bei 175° 30 Min. backen.

Zuletzt die Preiselbeeren und und die Schlagsahne auf den Kuchen streichen.

Gentlemans Cake (Herrentorte)

Ingredients:

Metric		Imperial	
200 g	coursely ground nuts	8 oz	coursely ground nuts
100 g	sugar	4 oz	sugar
4	egg yolks	4	egg yolks
125 g	margarine	5 oz	margarine
2 t	baking powder	2 t	baking powder
2-3 drops	almond extract	2-3 drops	almond extract
2 T	cocoa	2 T	cocoa
1 small can	cranberries	1 small can	cranberries
250 ml	whipping cream	1/2 pint	whipping cream

Method:

Cream sugar, egg yolks and margarine. Blend in cocoa, nuts, baking powder and almond extract. Whisk egg whites until they form very stiff peaks. Pour into greased and floured 20 cm (8 inch) spring-form baking tin. Bake in preheated oven at 175° C (350° F) for about 30 minutes or until skewer, inserted into centre of cake, comes out clean. Turn out on to rack and let cool. Spread cranberries over top of cake and then top with whipped cream.

Prinz - Eugen - Torte

Zutaten:

- 70 g Butter oder Margarine
- 5 Eigelb
- 80 g Zucker
- 1 P. Vanillezucker
- 150 g geh. Mandeln
- 1-2 Tr. Bittermandel
- 200 g Bitterschokol.
- 1 Eßl. Rum
- 1 Eßl. Cognac
- 1 Msp. Backpulver
- 5 Eiweiß

Zubereitung:

Fett schaumig rühren; Eigelb, Zucker, Vanillenzucker und eine Prise Salz nacheinander hinzufügen und so lange rühren, bis eine lockere Masse entstanden ist. Dann Mandeln, Bittermandel, 150 g aufgelöste Schokolade, Rum und Cognac daruntermischen. Backpulver und das steifgeschlagene Eiweiß unterheben.

Prince Eugéne Cake (Prinz - Eugen -Torte)

Ingredients:

Metric		Imperial	
70 g	butter or margarine	2 1/2 oz	butter or margarine
5	egg yolks	5	egg yolks
80 g	sugar	3 oz	sugar
1 t	vanilla extract	1 t	vanilla extract
1 pinch	salt	1 pinch	salt
150 g	ground almonds	6 oz	ground almonds
1-2 drops	almond extract	1-2 drops	almond extract
150 g	plain chocolate	6 oz	plain chocolate
1 T	rum	1 T	rum
1 T	cognac	1 T	cognac
1 pinch	baking powder	1 pinch	baking powder
5	egg whites	5	egg whites

Filling:
250 ml	whipping cream	8 fl oz	whipping cream
50 g	plain chocolate chips	2 oz	plain chocolate chips

Method:
Cream shortening, egg yolks and sugar; add vanilla and a pinch of salt. Whisk until light and creamy.

Den Teig in eine am Boden gefettete, mit Pergament ausgelegte Springform (∅ 26 cm) füllen und im vorgeheiztem Backofen auf der mittleren Schiene bei 150° etwa 50 Min. backen.

Für die Füllung ¼ l Sahne mit einem Päckchen Sahnefestiger steif schlagen. Restliche Schokolade raspeln, unter die Sahne mischen und die Masse gleichmäßig auf den abgekühlten Boden streichen.

Torte kalt stellen und evtl. mit Mokkabohnen oder Borkenschokolade verzieren.

Add ground nuts, almond extract, melted chocolate, rum and cognac. Fold in baking powder and stiffly beaten egg whites. Pour into greased and floured 25 cm (10 inch) spring-form baking tin. Bake in preheated oven at 150° C (300° F) for approx. 50 minutes or until skewer, inserted into centre of cake, comes out clean. Turn out onto rack and let cool.

Filling:
Whip cream blend in chocolate chips/flakes and cover cake. Chill before serving.

Himmelstorte

Zutaten:
- 100 g Butter
- 125 g Zucker
- 4 Eigelb
- 150 g Mehl
- 1/2 P. Backpulver

Belag:
- 4 Eiweiß
- 200 g Zucker
- 1 P. geh. Mandeln

Füllung:
- 1 Gl. Stachelbeeren oder Sauerkirschen
- 1/2 l Sahne

Zubereitung:
Aus den angegebenen Zutaten einen Teig rühren und auf 2 Böden verteilen.
Das Eiweiß und den Zucker zu steifem Schnee schlagen, auf beide Böden streichen. Dann die gehobelten Mandeln darüber streuen.

Heavens Cake (Himmelstorte)

Ingredients:

Metric		Imperial	
100 g	butter	4 oz	butter
125 g	sugar	5 oz	sugar
4	egg yolks	4	egg yolks
150 g	flour	6 oz	flour
1 t	baking powder	1 t	baking powder

Topping:
4	egg whites	4	egg whites
200 g	sugar	8 oz	sugar
200 g	coursely ground almonds	8 oz	coursely ground almonds

Filling:
1 jar (750 g)	gooseberries or sour cherries, drained	1 1/2 lbs	gooseberries or sour cherries, drained
500 ml	single whipping cream	1 pint	single whipping cream

Method:

Cream butter, sugar and egg yolks. Blend in sifted flour and baking powder. Pour into two greased and floured 18 cm (7 inch) baking tins.

Die Böden müssen sofort gebacken werden.
Backzeit: 30 Min. bei 175°
Einen Boden nach dem Backen sofort in Stücke schneiden, da dies in kaltem Zustand sehr schlecht geht. Nach dem Erkalten die Stachelbeeren mit Tortenguß binden und auf den Boden geben. 1/2 l Sahne sehr steif schlagen und über die Stachelbeeren streichen. Nun den in Stücke geschnittenen Boden auf die Sahne setzen.

Bake in a preheated oven at 175° C (350° F) for about 30 minutes or until skewer, inserted into centre of cake, comes out clean. Turn out onto rack to cool. Cut one base into pieces while still hot. Once the cake has cooled, thicken the gooseberries or cherries and sauce with some gelatine and spread over the still whole cake base. Whip cream and spread over cake. Arrange the cut cake pieces over cream.

Westfälischer Apfelkuchen

Zutaten:
- 250 g Butter o. Margar.
- 220 g Zucker
- 5 Eier
- 2 Tropf. Zitronenaroma
- 275 g Mehl
- 2 Teel. Backpulver

Füllung u. Guß:
- 1 kg feste, säuerl. Äpfel
- Rosinen
- 2 Eßl. Aprikosenmarmelade
- 2 Eßl. Wasser
- Mandelblättchen

Zubereitung:
Aus den Zutaten einen Rührteig bereiten. Die Hälfte davon in eine gefettete Springform ⌀ 26 geben und glattstreichen. Äpfel schälen und in Scheiben schneiden und in Lagen gemischt mit Rosinen daraufschichten. Den Restteig daraufgeben.

Apple Cake Westphalian Style (Westfälischer Apfelkuchen)

Ingredients:

Metric		Imperial	
250 g	butter or margarine	10 oz	butter or margarine
220 g	sugar	9 oz	sugar
5	eggs	5	eggs
	some lemon juice		some lemon juice
275 g	plain flour	11 oz	plain flour
2 t	baking powder	2 t	baking powder

Filling and topping:

1 kg	firm, sour apples	2 lbs	firm, sour apples
	raisins		raisins
2 T	apricot jam	2 T	apricot jam
2 T	water	2 T	water
	flaked almonds		flaked almonds

Method:

Cream butter, sugar, eggs, and lemon juice. Fold in sifted flour and baking powder. Pour half of mixture into greased and floured 25 cm (10 inch) spring-form baking tin. Spread smooth. Peel, core and slice apples and mix with raisins.

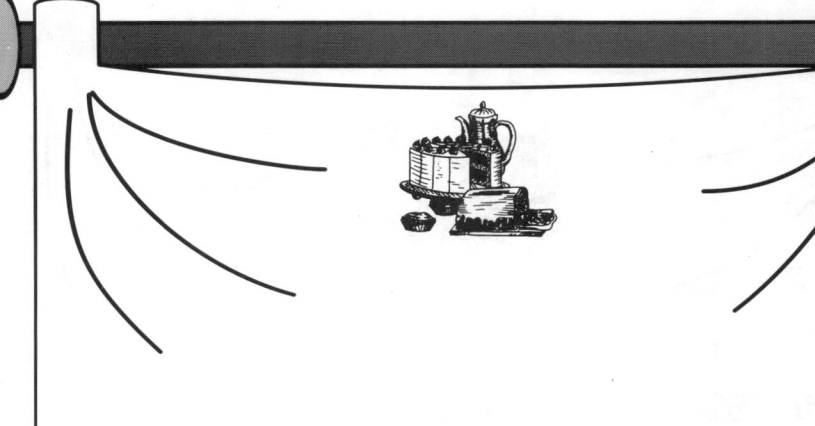

Bei 180° ca. 65 Min. backen. Aprikosenmarmelade durch ein Sieb geben, mit Wasser aufkochen und den Kuchen, wenn er noch warm ist, damit bestreichen und mit den Mandelblättchen verzieren und erkalten lassen.

Spread evenly over batter. Pour in the rest of batter. Bake in a preheated oven at 180° C (350° F) for approx. 65 minutes.

Strain apricot jam through a fine sieve; bring with water to the boil. Spread over entire cake whilst still hot and decorate with almond flakes.

Brauner Kirschkuchen

Zutaten:
- 140 g Butter o. Margar.
- 140 g Zucker
- 4 Eier
- 80 g Schokolade
- 50 g Semmelmehl
- 150 g gem. Mandeln
- 250 g Kirschen

Zubereitung:

Eier trennen und Eigelb mit Butter und Zucker schaumig rühren, geriebene Schokolade dazu geben. Semmelmehl und Mandeln mischen und abwechselnd mit Eischnee unter die Masse rühren. Teig in gefettete 22 ⌀ Springform geben. Entsteinte, gut abgetropfte Kirschen darauf geben.
Den Kuchen im vorgeheizten Backofen bei 175 - 200° ca. 50 - 60 Min. backen.

Brown Cherry Cake (Brauner Kirschkuchen)

Ingredients:

Metric		Imperial	
140 g	butter or margarine	6 oz	butter or margarine
140 g	sugar	6 oz	sugar
4	eggs, separated	4	eggs, separated
80 g	plain chocolate, grated	3 oz	plain chocolate, grated
50 g	fine breadcrumbs	2 oz	fine breadcrumbs
150 g	ground almonds	6 oz	ground almonds
250 g	cherries, stoned	10 oz	cherries, stoned

Method:

Cream egg yolks, sugar and butter; add grated chocolate. Mix breadcrumbs with ground almonds and blend into egg yolk cream, alternating with stiffly beaten egg whites. Pour into greased and floured 22 cm (9 inch) spring-form baking tin. Spread cherries over batter. Bake in preheated oven at 175° - 200° C (350° - 400° F) for 50 - 60 minutes.

Kirschkäsekuchen

Zutaten:

125	g	Mehl
2	Eßl.	Zucker
1	P.	Vanillezucker
1	Pr.	Salz
3	Eßl.	Milch
60	g	Butter oder Margarine
2	Tl.	Zitronensaft
1		Ei
75	g	Mehl
3	Tl.	Backpulver

Füllung:

1	P.	Vanillepudding
4	Eßl.	Zucker
1/2	l	Milch
1		Eigelb
1		Eiweiß
250	g	Quark
1/2	Fl.	Rum-Aroma
1	D.	Sauerkirschen

Zubereitung:

Mehl mit Zucker und Vanillezucker und Salz mischen. Im Topf Milch

Cheese and Cherry Cake (Kirschkäsekuchen)

Ingredients:

Metric   **Imperial**

Base:
125 g	plain flour	5 oz	plain flour
2 T	sugar	2 T	sugar
1 t	vanilla extract	1 t	vanilla extract
1 pinch	salt	1 pinch	salt
3 T	milk	3 T	milk
60 g	butter or margarine	2 1/2 oz	butter or margarine
2 t	lemon juice	2 t	lemon juice
1	egg	1	egg
75 g	plain flour	3 oz	plain flour
3 t	baking powder	3 t	baking powder

Filling:
50 g	custard powder	2 oz	custard powder
4 T	sugar	4 T	sugar
500 ml	milk	1 pint	milk
1	egg yolk	1	egg yolk
1	egg white	1	egg white
250 g	curd	10 oz	curd
1-2 T	rum	1-2 T	rum
750 g	sour cherries, stoned	1 1/2 lbs	sour cherries, stoned

und Fett erhitzen bis das Fett geschmolzen ist, Zitronensaft zugeben. Diese Flüssigkeit (leicht geronnen) von der Mitte aus in die Mehlmischung rühren, Ei zugeben und Teig abkühlen lassen. Das übrige Mehl mit Backpulver mischen und unter den Teig schlagen. Den Teig in eine 26 Ø Springform füllen und glattstreichen. Vanillepudding nach Vorschrift kochen. Das steifgeschlagene Eiweiß unter den heißen Pudding ziehen. Quark durch ein Sieb streichen, Rum-Aroma untermischen und alles mit dem Pudding vermischen. Die Hälfte der Creme auf den Teig geben, abgetropfte Kirschen darauf verteilen und restliche Creme darübergeben.
Den Kuchen auf der mittleren Schiene in mittlerer Hitze bei 200° ca. 60 Min. im vorgeheizten Ofen backen.
Gesüßte Schlagsahne dazu reichen.

Method:

Base:

Mix 125 g (5 oz) flour, sugar, vanilla and salt in a mixing bowl; make a well in the centre. Heat milk and butter in saucepan and add lemon juice. Pour into centre of flour mixture. Mix well, adding egg. Leave dough to cool. Mix the rest of flour with baking powder and beat into the dough. Turn out dough into 25 cm (10 inch) springform baking tin and smooth down.

Filling:

Prepare custard according to cooking instructions. Fold in stiffly beaten egg whites. Whisk curd, add rum and mix with custard. Spread half of the filling on top of dough base, add drained cherries, then pour over the rest of custard cream. Bake in preheated oven at 200° C (400° F) for about 60 minutes. Remove from tin to cool. Serve with sweetened whipped cream.

Käsekuchen

Zutaten:
- 75 g Margarine
- 75 g Zucker
- 1 Ei
- 200 g Mehl
- 1 Teel. Backpulver

Belag:
- 500 g Magerquark
- 150 g Zucker
- 1 Ei
- 2 Eigelb
- 1 P. Sahnepudding
- 1 P. Vanillezucker
- 1/2 Fl. Bittermandel
- 1/2 Fl. Arrak
- 1 Tasse Öl
- 1 Prise Salz
- 1/2 l Milch

Zubereitung:

Den Knetteig aus den obigen Zutaten in eine Springform geben und ca. 4 cm Rand hochdrücken. Dann die Belag-Flüssigkeit einfüllen.

Cheese Cake (Käsekuchen)

Ingredients:

Metric		Imperial	

To make dough:
75 g	butter or margarine	3 oz	butter or margarine
75 g	sugar	3 oz	sugar
1	egg	1	egg
200 g	flour	8 oz	flour
1 t	baking powder	1 t	baking powder

To make filling:
500 g	low fat curd	1 lb	low fat curd
150 g	sugar	6 oz	sugar
1	egg	1	egg
2	egg yolks	2	egg yolks
50 g	custard powder	2 oz	custard powder
1/2 t	vanilla extract	1/2 t	vanilla extract
2-3 drops	almond extract	2-3 drops	almond extract
1 T	rum or arrak	1 T	rum or arrak
125 -250 ml	cooking oil	4-8 fl oz	cooking oil
1 pinch	salt	1 pinch	salt
500 ml	milk	1/2 pint	milk

Bei 200° 60 Min. backen.
Die 2 Eiweiß mit 2 Eßl. Zucker
zu Schnee schlagen und den Kuchen
dann bestreichen und noch
weitere 10 Min. überbacken.

Method:

Beat and knead all dough ingredients to make a smooth dough. Line greased 20 to 22 cm (8 to 9 inch) springform baking tin with dough, making a rim of about 4 cm (1-2 inches).

Blend all filling ingredients to a smooth cream. Pour into dough casing. Bake in a preheated oven at 200° C (400° F) for about 60 minutes. Whisk 2 egg whites and 2 T castor sugar until they form stiff peaks. Spread over cake and bake for another 10 minutes.

Quarkstollen

Zutaten:

- 500 g Mehl
- 1 P. Backpulver
- 1 Teel. Honigkuchengewürz
- 2 Eier
- 175 g Zucker
- 1 P. Vanillezucker
- 3 Tr. Backöl Zitrone
- 200 g Margarine
- 250 g Magerquark
- 250 g Rosinen
- 65 g Orangeat
- 125 g gem. Mandeln
- 2-3 Eßl. Rum

Zubereitung:

Das Gemisch aus Mehl, Backpulver und Honigkuchengewürz mit Eiern, Zucker, Vanillezucker, Backöl, in Stückchen geschnittener Margarine, trockenem Quark, gewaschenen Rosinen, gehacktem Orangeat, Mandeln und Rum zu einem Teig

Fruit Loaf - also known in the USA as Stollen (Quarkstollen)

Ingredients:

Metric		Imperial	
500 g	plain flour	1 lb	plain flour
30 g	baking powder	1 oz	baking powder
1 t	ginger bread spices, ground	1 t	ginger bread spices, ground
1	egg	1	egg
175 g	sugar	7 oz	sugar
1 t	vanilla extract	1 t	vanilla extract
grated rind of one untreated lemon		grated rind of one untreatd lemon	
some lemon juice		some lemon juice	
200 g	margarine	8 oz	margarine
250 g	low fat curd	10 oz	low fat curd
250 g	seedless raisins	10 oz	seedless raisins
65 g	candied orange peel	2 1/2 oz	candied orange peel
125 g	ground almonds	5 oz	ground almonds
2-3 T	rum	2-3 T	rum

verarbeiten.
Im Gegensatz zu einem Hefe-
stollen muß der Teig rasch ver-
knetet werden. Zu einem Stollen
formen; auf ein gefettetes, bemehltes
Backblech legen und bei 150° etwa
75 Min. goldbraun backen.
Noch heiß mit zerlassener Butter
bestreichen und mit Puderzucker
bestäuben.

Method:

Quickly beat and knead all ingredients in given order to a smooth dough. Form a loaf (stollen). Put onto a greased baking tray and bake in preheated oven at 150°C (300° F) for 75 minutes until golden brown. Remove from oven and place on serving platter. Pour over melted butter and then dust well with powdered sugar.

Terrassen-Kuchen

Zutaten:

250	g	Butter oder Margarine
200	g	Zucker
1		abgeriebene Zitronenschale
4		Eier
150	g	Mehl
100	g	Speisestärke
3	Eßl.	Kakao
3	Teel.	Backpulver

Füllung u. Guß:

200	g	aufgelöste Zartbitter-Schokolade
2-3	Eßl.	Aprikosenmarmelade
250	g	Puderzucker
4	Eßl.	Orangensaft

Zubereitung:
Aus den angegebenen Zutaten einen Rührteig bereiten und auf ein gefettetes Blech streichen.

Terraced Cake (Terrassen-Kuchen)

Ingredients:

Metric		Imperial	
Batter:			
250 g	butter or margarine	1/2 lb	butter or margarine
200 g	sugar	8 oz	sugar
grated rind of 1 untreated lemon		grated rind of 1 untreated lemon	
4	eggs	4	eggs
150 g	flour	6 oz	flour
100 g	corn starch	4 oz	corn starch
3 T	cocoa	3 T	cocoa
3 t	baking powder	3 t	baking powder
Filling and Glaze:			
200 g	melted plain chocolate	8 oz	melted plain chocolate
2-3 T	apricot jam	2-3 T	apricot jam
250 g	icing sugar	1/2 lb	icing sugar
4 T	orange juice	4 T	orange juice
	candied cherries (optional)		candied cherries (optional)

Method:

Cream butter, sugar and eggs. Blend in sifted flour, cocoa, corn starch and baking powder. Continue whisking to make a light and creamy batter.

Im vorgeheitzten Backofen bei 200 – 225° ca. 15 – 20 Min. abbacken. Kuchen in 4 verschieden breite Streifen schneiden. Breitesten Streifen auf die Platte legen. Die anderen Streifen auf der Unterseite mit Aprikosenmarmelade und Schokoladenmasse bestreichen und terrassenförmig aufeinanderschichten.
Mit Guß aus Orangensaft und Puderzucker überziehen und evtl. mit kandierten Kirschen verzieren.

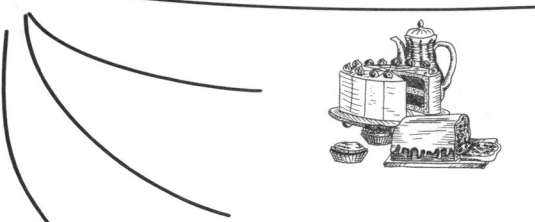

Pour into greased and floured 4.2 cm (17 inch) baking tray, spread evenly. Bake in preheated oven at 200°-225° C (400°- 425° F) for 15-20 minutes.
Cut cake into 4 strips of differing width. Put broadest strip on platter. Spread the undersides of the remaining strips with apricot jam and melted chocolate. Place on top of each other to form a terraced tower. Mix well icing sugar and orange juice and glaze terraced cake. Garnish with candied cherries.

Ananas-Kuchen

Zutaten:

1	D.	Ananas (585ml) in Stücken
200	g	Butter
175	g	Zucker
1	P.	Vanillinzucker
4		Eier
1		unbeh. Zitrone
250	g	Mehl
50	g	Speisestärke
1/2	P.	Backpulver
1	Pr.	Salz
200	g	Puderzucker
4	Eßl.	Ananassaft

Zubereitung:

Ananas abtropfen, Saft auffangen. Butter, Zucker, Vanillinzucker und Eier schaumig rühren, Schale der Zitrone hineinreiben. Mehl, Speisestärke und Backpulver mischen und unterrühren; Ananasstücke (evtl. etwas kleiner geschnitten) unterheben, einige Stücke zum

Pineapple Cake (Ananas-Kuchen)

Ingredients:

Metric		Imperial	
1 large can pineapple chunks, drained		1 large can pineapple chunks, drained	
200 g	butter	8 oz	butter
175 g	sugar	7 oz	sugar
1/2 t	vanilla extract	1/2 t	vanilla extract
4	eggs	4	eggs
grated rind of one untreated lemon		grated rind of one untreated lemon	
250 g	plain flour	1/2 lb	plain flour
50 g	corn starch	2 oz	corn starch
2 t	baking powder	2 t	baking powder
1 pinch	salt	1 pinch	salt
200 g	icing sugar	8 oz	icing sugar
4 T	pineapple juice	4 T	pineapple juice

Method:

If necessary, cut pineapple into smaller pieces. Cream butter, sugar, vanilla and eggs. Add lemon rind, fold in sifted flour, corn starch and baking powder. Blend well. Add pineapple chunks. Retain some chunks for garnishing. Pour batter into greased and floured loaf tin.

Verzieren zurückbehalten. Teig in eine gefettete 30 cm - Kastenform einfüllen. Im vorgeheizten Backofen bei 175° auf unterer Schiene ca. 60 Min. backen. Nach 15 Min. Backzeit Teig einschneiden, damit er gleichmäßig reißt.
Puderzucker mit 4 EßI. Saft glattrühren, den noch warmen Kuchen damit überziehen und mit den restlichen Ananasstückchen verzieren.

Bake in preheated oven at 175° C (350° F) for 60 minutes or until skewer, inserted into centre of cake, comes out clean. Make a slit in cake after 15 minutes of baking. This will assure even baking. Invert cake onto cooling rack.

Mix icing sugar and pineapple juice to make a glaze. Paint still warm cake with glaze and decorate with pineapple chunks.

Nußkuchen

Zutaten:

250	g	Butter oder Margarine
250	g	Zucker
3		Eier
200	g	gem. Nüsse
125	g	Blockschokolade
375	g	Mehl
1	P.	Backpulver
1	T.	Milch oder
4	Eßl.	Rum
		Schokoladenglasur

Zubereitung:
Butter und Zucker schaumig rühren, nach und nach die Eier dazugeben, dann die Nüsse und die Schokolade. Zuletzt Mehl, Backpulver und Milch.
Auf den abgekühlten Kuchen die Schokoladenglasur streichen.
Bei 200° 60 Min. backen.

Nut Cake (Nußkuchen)

Ingredients:

Metric		Imperial	
250 g	butter or margarine	1/2 lb	butter or margarine
250 g	sugar	1/2 lb	sugar
3	eggs	3	eggs
200 g	ground almonds and hazelnuts	8 oz	ground almonds and hazelnuts
125 g	plain chocolate, flaked	5 oz	plain chocolate, flaked
375 g	plain flour	15 oz	plain flour
4-5 t	baking powder	4-5 t	baking powder
	milk or 4 T rum		milk or 4 T rum
	chocolate glaze		chocolate glaze

Method:

Cream butter and sugar. Whisk in eggs. Add grated nuts and chocolate. Blend in sifted flour and baking powder. Add enough milk or 4 T rum, whilst beating to make a creamy batter. Pour into greased and floured loaf tin. Bake at 200° (400° F) for 60 minutes or until skewer, inserted into centre of cake, comes out clean. Turn out onto rack and let cool. Glaze.

Gold und Silber

Zutaten:

Gold:
- 5 Eigelb
- 150 g Margarine
- 180 g Zucker
- 250 g Mehl
- ½ P. Backpulver
- ½ Ta. Milch

Silber:
- 5 Eiweiß
- 150 g Margarine
- 250 g Zucker
- 125 g gem. Nüsse
- 250 g Mehl
- ½ Ta. Milch
- ½ P. Backpulver

Zubereitung:

Von den Zutaten für Gold der Reihe nach einen Rührteig herstellen und in eine Springform füllen.
Für Silber Eiweiß steif schlagen, aus den anderen Zutaten einen zweiten Rührteig herstellen und steifes Eiweiß unterheben. In die Form auf den Goldteig geben.

50 - 60 Min. bei 175° - 200° backen.

Gold and Silver (Gold und Silber)

Ingredients:

Metric		Imperial	
Gold			
5	egg yolks	5	egg yolks
150 g	margarine	6 oz	margarine
180 g	sugar	7 oz	sugar
250 g	flour	1/2 lb	flour
2-3 t	baking powder	2-3 t	baking powder
1/2 cup	milk	1/2 cup	milk
Silver			
5	egg whites	5	egg whites
150 g	margarine	6 oz	margarine
250 g	sugar	1/2 lb	sugar
125 g	ground almonds or hazelnuts	5 oz	ground almonds or hazelnuts
250 g	flour	1/2 lb	flour
1/2 cup	milk	1/2 cup	milk
2-3 t	baking powder	2-3 t	baking powder

Method:

Gold: In given order, mix all ingredients to a smooth batter. Pour into greased and floured 25 cm (10 inch) spring-form baking tin.

Silver: Whisk egg whites until the form stiff peaks. Cream remaining ingredients, fold in egg whites. Pour on top of Gold batter. Bake in preheated oven at $175°$-$200°$ C ($350°$-$400°$ F) for 50-60 minutes or until skewer, inserted into centre of cake, comes out clean.

Rotweinkuchen

Zutaten:

- 200 g Butter
- 200 g Zucker
- 1 P. Vanillezucker
- 4 Eier (Eigelb u. Eiweiß getrennt)
- 100 g grobe Schokostr.
- 1 Teel. Zimt
- 1 Teel. Kakao
- 250 g Mehl
- 3/4 P. Backpulver
- 1/8 l Rotwein

Zubereitung:

Butter, Zucker und Eigelb schaumig rühren. Mehl, Backpulver und Gewürze zugeben. und Rotwein unterrühren. Zum Schluß Eischnee und Schokostreusel.

45 Min. bei 180° backen.

Red Wine Cake (Rotweinkuchen)

Ingredients:

Metric		Imperial	
200 g	butter	8 oz	butter
200 g	sugar	8 oz	sugar
1 t	vanilla extract	1 t	vanilla extract
4	eggs, separated	4	eggs, separated
100 g	course chocolate flakes	4 oz	course chocolate flakes
1 t	cinnamon	1 t	cinnamon
1 t	cocoa	1 t	cocoa
250 g	flour	1/2 oz	flour
3 t	baking powder	3 t	baking powder
125 ml	red wine	4 fl oz	red wine

Method:

Cream, butter, sugar and egg yolks. Blend in flour, baking powder and spices. Whisk in red wine. Fold in stiffly beaten egg whites and chocolate chips. Pour into greased and floured loaf tin. Bake in preheated oven at 180° C (350° F) for 45 minutes or until skewer, inserted into centre of cake, comes out clean. Turn out onto rack to cool.

Napoleon – Kuchen

Zutaten:
- 300 g Margarine
- 300 g Zucker
- 1 P. Vanillezucker
- 7 Eigelb
- 150 g gem. Mandeln
- 150 g Schokoladenstr.
- 1 Fl. Rum-Aroma
- 1 Fl. Arrak-Aroma
- 150 g Mehl
- 1 P. Backpulver
- 7 Eiweiß zu Schnee schlagen

Guß:
- 250 g Puderzucker
- 50 g Kakao
- 3 Eßl. heißes Wasser
- 2 Würfel Palmin

Zubereitung:
Alle Zutaten in einer Schüssel gut verrühren und Eischnee unterheben. In einer 30-Springform bei 180° 70 Min. abbacken. Den Guß ganz glatt auftragen.

Napoleon Cake (Napoleon - Kuchen)

Ingredients:

Metric		Imperial	
300 g	margarine	12 oz	margarine
300 g	sugar	12 oz	sugar
1/2 t	vanilla extract	1/2 t	vanilla extract
7	eggs, seperated	7	eggs, seperated
150 g	grated almonds	6 oz	grated almonds
150 g	chocolate chips	6 oz	chocolate chips
2 T	rum	2 T	rum
150 g	flour	6 oz	flour
4 t	baking powder	4 t	baking powder

Glaze:
250 g	icing sugar	1/2 lb	icing sugar
50 g	cocoa	2 oz	cocoa
3 T	hot water	3 T	hot water
	shortening		shortening

Method:

Briskly mix all batter ingredients. Fold in stiffly beaten egg whites. Bake in greased and floured loaf tin at 180°C/350°F for 70 minutes. Turn out onto rack to cool. Glaze.

Bananen-Gewürzkuchen

Zutaten:
- 250 g Margarine
- 250 g Zucker
- 300 g Mehl
- 3-4 Bananen (zerkleinern)
- 1/2 Teel. Natron
- 1/2 P. Backpulver
- 1 Teel. Zimt
- 1/2 Teel. gem. Nelken
- 1 Msp. gem. Muskat
- 2 Eßl. Kakao
- 100 g Bitter Schokol.
- 2 Eßl. Rum

Zubereitung:
Aus den Zutaten wie angegeben einen Rührteig herstellen.
Der Kuchen kann 2 Tage vor Anschnitt gebacken werden.

60 Min. bei 200° backen.

Banana Spicy Cake (Bananen-Gewürzkuchen)

Ingredients:

Metric		Imperial	
250 g	margarine	1/2 lb	margarine
250 g	sugar	1/2 lb	sugar
300 g	flour	12 oz	flour
3-4	bananas, peeled and diced	3-4	bananas, peeled and diced
1/2 t	soda	1/2 t	soda
2 t	baking powder	2 t	baking powder
1 t	cinnamon	1 t	cinnamon
1/2 t	grated cloves	1/2 t	grated cloves
1/4 t	grated nutmeg	1/4 t	grated nutmeg
2 T	cocoa	2 t	cocoa
100 g	plain chocolate, grated	4 oz	plain chocolate, grated
2 T	rum	2 T	rum

Method:

Cream all ingredients other than bananas and chocolate. Stir in bananas and chocolate.

Pour into greased and floured loaf tin. Bake in preheated oven at 200°C/400°F for 60 minutes or until a skewer, inserted into centre, of the cake, comes out clean.

Bananenkuchen

Zutaten:

- 125 g Butter oder Margarine
- 150 g Zucker
- 1 P. Vanillezucker
- 1 Prise Salz
- 2 Eier
- 200 g. Mehl
- 1 P. Vanillepudding
- 4 Teel. Backpulver
- 1 Eßl. Milch
- gehackte Mandeln
- 3 reife Bananen

Zubereitung:

Butter, Zucker, Vanillezucker und Salz schaumig rühren. Eier quirlen und dazugeben. Mehl, Puddingpulver und Backpulver unterrühren. Danach die Milch, gehackte Mandeln und die Bananen zerdrückt untermischen. Eine Kastenform mit Pergamentpapier auslegen. Bei ca. 175° 60 Min abbacken.

Banana Cake (Bananenkuchen)

Ingredients:

Metric		Imperial	
125 g	butter or margarine	5 oz	butter or margarine
125 g	sugar	5 oz	sugar
1/2 t	vanilla extract	1/2 t	vanilla extract
1 pinch	salt	1 pinch	salt
2	eggs	2	eggs
200 g	flour	8 oz	flour
50 g	custard powder	2 oz	custard powder
4 t	baking powder	4 t	baking powder
1 T	milk	1 T	milk
	chopped almonds		chopped almonds
3	ripe bananas	3	ripe bananas

Method:

Beat butter, sugar, vanilla extract and salt until light and creamy. Beat in whisked eggs. Gradually add sifted flour, custard powder and baking powder. Mix well. Peel and mash bananas. Add milk, chopped almonds and mashed bananas to batter. Line a loaf tin with grease proof paper. Pour in batter and bake in preheated oven at 175°C/350°F for 60 minutes or until skewer, inserted into centre of cake, comes out clean. Turn out onto rack to cool.

Ananas - Marzipan-Kuchen

Zutaten:
- 200 g Marzipanrohmasse
- 175 g Butter oder Margarine
- 175 g Zucker
- 1 P. Vanillezucker
- 3 Eier
- 300 g Mehl
- 2 Teel. Backpulver
- 2 Scheiben Ananas oder Ananasstücke

Zubereitung:

Marzipanrohmasse in kleine Streifen schneiden und mit dem Fett schaumig rühren. Zucker, Vanillezucker und Eier einrühren und das mit Backpulver gemischte Mehl unterziehen. Die gewürfelten Ananasscheiben unterheben.

Teig in eine gefettete Kastenform füllen und bei 200° ca. 60 - 70 Min. backen.

Pineapple Marzipan Cake (Ananas-Marzipan-Kuchen)

Ingredients:

Metric		Imperial	
200 g	marzipan	8 oz	marzipan
175 g	butter or margarine	7 oz	butter or margarine
175 g	sugar	7 oz	sugar
1/2 t	vanilla extract	1/2 t	vanilla extract
3	eggs	3	eggs
300 g	flour	12 oz	flour
2 t	baking powder	2 t	baking powder
2	slices pineapple	2	slices pineapple
(or equal amount in chunks)		(or equal amount in chunks)	

Method:

Cut marzipan into small strips. Whisk well with butter until creamy. Add sugar, vanilla extract and eggs. Keep on beating. Fold in sifted flour and baking powder. Stir in pineapple chunks. Put batter in a greased and floured loaf tin and bake in a preheated oven at 200°C/400°F for about 60-70 minutes or until a skewer, inserted into centre of cake, comes out clean.

Stachelbeerkuchen

Zutaten:

1/2		ungespritze Zitrone
200	g	Butter
200	g	Zucker
2		Eier
4		Eigelb
500	g	Mehl
1/2	P.	Backpulver
		etwas Milch

Belag: 1 1/2 kg Stachelbeeren gefroren

Guß:

4		Eiweiß
200	g	Zucker
100	g	Mandeln
1	Eßl.	Speisestärke
		Zitronenschale

Zubereitung:
Einen sehr steifen Rührteig aus den angegebenen Zutaten bereiten, mit den Stachelbeeren belegen. (Es können auch eingekochte, gut abgetropfte Stachelbeeren sein). Bei 190-200° ca. 45-50 Min. backen. Nach 1/2 Backzeit Guß drauf.

Gooseberry Cake (Stachelbeerkuchen)

Ingredients:

Metric		Imperial	
Batter:			
1/2	untreated lemon	1/2	untreated lemon
200 g	butter	8 oz	butter
200 g	sugar	8 oz	sugar
2	eggs	2	eggs
4	egg yolks	4	egg yolks
500 g	flour	1 lb	flour
2 t	baking powder	2 t	baking powder
	some milk		some milk
1 1/2 kg	frozen gooseberries	3 lb	frozen gooseberries

 (or equivalent amount of very well drained canned gooseberries)

Topping:

4	egg whites	4	egg whites
200 g	sugar	8 oz	sugar
100 g	grated almonds	4 oz	grated almonds
1 T	corn starch	1 T	corn starch

grated rind of one untreated lemon   grated rind of one untreated lemon

Method:

Cream all batter ingredients well. Pour into greased and floured spring-form baking tin. Spread gooseberries over batter. Bake in preheated oven at 190°-200°C /375°-400°F for 25 minutes. Whisk egg whites and sugar until stiff peaks form. Fold in grated almonds, starch and lemon rind. Remove cake from oven and cover with egg white mixture. Return to oven and bake for another 20-25 minutes. Remove from tin to cool.

Schüttelkuchen

Zutaten:
- 300 g Mehl
- 300 g Zucker
- 180 g gem. Nüsse
- 180 g Schokoladenstr.
- 1 P. Backpulver
- 1 P. Vanillezucker
- 3 Eier
- 1/4 l kalten Kaffee
- 1 EBl. Rum

Zubereitung:
Zuerst alle flüssigen Zutaten in eine Schüssel geben. Die restlichen Zutaten darauf; und zuletzt das Mehl. Schüssel gut verschließen und kräftig schütteln!

60 Min. bei 180° backen.

Shaked Cake (Schüttelkuchen)

Ingredients:

Metric   _Imperial_

300 g	flour	12 oz	flour
300 g	sugar	12 oz	sugar
180 g	grated nuts (hazelnuts or almonds)	7 oz	grated nuts (hazelnuts or almonds)
180 g	plain chocolate chips	7 oz	plain chocolate chips
1/2 t	vanilla extract	1/2 t	vanilla extract
3	eggs	3	eggs
250 ml	cold coffee	1/2 pint	cold coffee
1 T	rum	1 T	rum

Method:

Put all liquid ingredients in a large bowl (which can be covered with a lid). Add all other ingredients (except flour), but do not stir! Finally, sifted flour on to other ingredients. Cover bowl with a lid and shake briskly. Pour into greased and floured loaf tin. Bake in preheated oven at 180°C/350°F for 60 minutes. A skewer, inserted into centre of the cake, has to come out clean when the cake is done.

Bio - Kuchen

Zutaten:

300	g	Roggenmehl
3	Eßl.	Honig
1		Ei
1	Msp.	Zimt
1	Msp.	gem. Nelken
1	Msp.	gem. Muskat
3	Eßl.	Leinsamen
1	Teel.	Kakao
1	P.	Trockenhefe
1	Eßl.	Pflanzenöl
10		Trockenpflaumen
1/8	l	Milch
1	Pr.	Salz

Zubereitung:
Pflaumen klein schneiden und mit den übrigen Zutaten nach Anweisung für Trockenhefe zu einem Teig verarbeiten. Diesen in eine gefettete Kastenform füllen und bei 175° ca. 30-40 Min. backen.
Für Diabetiker gut geeignet.

Bio Cake (Bio-Kuchen)

Ingredients:

Metric		Imperial	
300 g	rye flour	12 oz	rye flour
3 T	honey	3 T	honey
1	egg	1	egg
1/4 t	cinnamon	1/4 t	cinnamon
1/4 t	ground cloves	1/4 t	ground cloves
1/2 t	ground nutmeg	1/2 t	ground nutmeg
3 T	lin seed	3 T	lin seed
1 t	cocoa	1 t	cocoa
1 cake	compressed yeast	1 cake	compressed yeast
(or equivalent in dried form)		(or equivalent in dried form)	
1 T	oil	1 T	oil
10	prunes, stoned and cut	10	prunes, stoned and cut
125 ml	hand hot milk	1/4 pint	hand hot milk
1 pinch	salt	1 pinch	salt

Method:

Dissolve 1 level teaspoon sugar in handhot milk in a small basin. Crumble or sprinkle in yeast and leave until frothy, about 10 minutes. Place flour, sugar, cocoa, oil and spices in the bowl. Mix together. Beat egg and salt together in a small basin. Add yeast liquid and egg to flour mixture. Beat thoroughly for 10 minutes, stretch the dough well. Blend in prune pieces. Cover bowl and let rise for about 1 hour or until dough has doubled in size. Put dough in a greased and floured loaf tin and bake in preheated oven at 175°C/350°F for 30-40 minutes.

Suitable for diabetics.

Kartoffelkuchen mit Hefe

Zutaten:
- 250 g Mehl
- 40 g Zucker
- 3 gek. Kartoffeln
- 60 g Butter
- etwas Salz
- Muskat
- 15 g Hefe
- 1 P. Vanillezucker

Zubereitung:
Aus den Zutaten einen Hefeteig bereiten. Den Teig auf dem Blech ausrollen und mit Butterflocken belegen. Nach dem Backen mit Zucker, Vanillezucker bestreuen.

Potato Yeast Cake (Kartoffelkuchen mit Hefe)

Ingredients:

Metric		Imperial	
250 g	flour	1/2 lb	flour
40 g	sugar	1 1/2 oz	sugar
3	pre-cooked potatoes	3	pre-cooked potatoes
60 g	butter	2 oz	butter
	some salt		some salt
	grated nutmeg		grated nutmeg
15 g	compressed yeast	1/2 oz	compressed yeast
1 pkt	vanilla sugar	1 pkt	vanilla extract
	flaked butter		flaked butter

Method:

Mix 1 teaspoon sugar with some (6-8 tablespoons) hand-hot milk in a small basin. Crumble in yeast. Cover and leave for some minutes until frothy. Melt butter and leave to cool. Peel and mash potatoes. Mix flour, sugar, mashed potatoes, salt and nutmeg. Add yeast mixture. Beat well to a smooth dough. Let rise in a covered bowl until dough has doubled in size. Roll out on a rectangular baking tray. Spread melted butter on dough. Sprinkle with vanilla sugar. Bake in preheated oven at 250°C/500°F for 25 minutes.

Pumpernickel - Kuchen

Zutaten:
- 100 g Butter oder Margarine
- 750 g Pumpernickel
- 4 Eßl. Zucker
- 100 g ger. Edelbitterschokolade
- 820 g Apfelmus
- 25 g Butter oder Margarine
- 1/8 l Sahne
- 1 Eßl. Himbeermarmelade

Zubereitung:
100 g Butter erhitzen, zerkrümelten Pumpernickel und Zucker hineingeben und 5 Min. gut verrühren. Schokolade dazugeben und unter Rühren schmelzen lassen, bis alles gut vermischt ist. Diese Masse 1 cm hoch in eine Ø 22 cm Springform geben und festdrücken, darauf Apfelmus geben und schichtweise weiter "Krümelmasse"

Pumpernickel Cake
(Pumpernickel-Kuchen)

Ingredients:

Metric		Imperial	
100 g	butter or margarine	4 oz	butter or margarine
750 g	pumpernickel	1 1/2 lb	pumpernickel
4 T	sugar	4 T	sugar
100 g	ground plain chocolate	4 oz	ground plain chocolate
820 g	apple-purée	33 oz	apple-purée
25 g	flaked butter	1 oz	flaked butter
125 ml	single cream	1/4 pint	single cream
1 T	raspberry jam	1 T	raspberry jam

Method:

Melt butter and add crumbled pumpernickel and sugar. Stir well over moderate heat for 5 minutes. Add ground chocolate and let melt while stirring continually. Grease and flour a 22 cm (9 inch) spring-form tin. Put some of the mixture into tin (about 1 cm/1/2 inch high).

und Apfelmus abwechseln (oberste Lage Krümel). 25g Fett in Flöckchen darauf setzen und bei 200° im vorgeheizten Ofen 30 Min. backen. Kuchen abkühlen lassen, Himbeermarmelade unter steifgeschlagene Sahne heben und damit den Kuchen verzieren.

Press into tin. Add apple-purée and rest of the mixture in alternating layers (the last layer should be pumpernickel mixture). Spread with flaked butter and bake in preheated oven at 200°C/400°F for 30 minutes. When cake is done, let cool down. Beat single cream until stiff. Fold in raspberry jam. Top cake with the mixture.

Omnibus

Zutaten:
- 250 g Margarine
- 5 Eier
- 500 g Zucker
- 500 g Mehl
- 1 P. Backpulver
- etwas Salz
- 1-2 T. Milch
- Zitronenschale
- Muskat

Zubereitung:

Margarine schaumig rühren, Zucker, Eigelb und die Gewürze hinzugeben. Dann das Mehl und die Milch, zuletzt das Backpulver unterrühren. Eischnee schlagen und vorsichtig unterheben.

Bei 175° 60 Min. backen.

Omnibus

Ingredients:

Metric		Imperial	
250 g	margarine	1/2 lb	margarine
5	eggs, seperated	5	eggs, seperated
500 g	sugar	1 lb	sugar
500 g	plain flour	1 lb	plain flour
4 t	baking powder	4 t	baking powder
	some salt		some salt
1-2 T	milk	1-2 T	milk
grated rind of one untreated lemon		grated rind of one untreated lemon	
ground nutmeg		ground nutmeg	

Method:
Beat margarine, sugar and egg yolks until light and creamy. Add lemon and nutmeg. Finally blend in sifted flour, baking powder and milk. Fold in stiffly beaten egg whites. Pour into greased and floured loaf tin. Bake in preheated oven at 175°C/350°F for 60 minutes or until skewer, inserted into centre of cake, comes out clean. Turn out onto rack to cool.

Ballettschnitten

Zutaten:
- 250 g Mehl
- 100 g Butter
- 125 g Zucker
- 2 Eigelb
- 1 Vanillezucker
- 1 Tl. Backpulver

Füllung:
- 125 g geh. Mandeln
- 65 g Butter
- 100 g Zucker
- 1 Eigelb
- 3 Eiweiß
- abger. Apfelsinenschale

Zubereitung:
Butter, Zucker und Eigelb schaumig rühren, Mandeln und Eischnee unterziehen und zum Schluß noch die abgeriebene Apfelsinenschale.
Aus dem Teig werden 3 Streifen ca.10cm breit ausgerollt und vorgebacken. Dann streicht man die Mandelmasse auf die Streifen, überbäckt sie nochmal und schneidet sie dann in 1cm breite Stücke.

Ballett Pieces (Ballettschnitten)

Ingredients:

Metric		Imperial	
Dough:			
250 g	flour	1/2 lb	flour
100 g	butter	4 oz	butter
125 g	sugar	5 oz	sugar
2	egg yolks	2	egg yolks
1/2 t	vanilla extract	1/2 t	vanilla extract
1 t	baking powder	1 t	baking powder
Filling:			
125 g	chopped almonds	5 oz	chopped almonds
65 g	butter	2 1/2 oz	butter
100 g	sugar	4 oz	sugar
1	egg yolk	1	egg yolk
3	egg whites	3	egg whites
grated rind of one untreated orange		grated rind of one untreated orange	

Method:

Mix all dough ingredients to make a smooth dough. Roll out and cut in 3 strips (10 cm/8 inches wide). Bake strips in preheated oven at 175°C/350°F for 10-15 minutes. Beat butter, sugar and egg yolks until light and creamy. Fold in stiffly beaten egg whites and chopped almonds. Finally blend in grated rind of one untreated orange. Spread over strips and bake for another 20-25 minutes. Remove from oven and cut into strips of 1 cm (1/2 inch).

Feine Waffeln

Zutaten:

6		Eigelb
300	g	Margarine
1	P.	Vanillezucker
1	Pr.	Zimt
3/8	l	Milch
130	g	Zucker
400	g	Mehl
1	P.	Backpulver

Zubereitung:

Alle Zutaten zu einem Rührteig mit dem Mixer verarbeiten. Eiweiß zum Schluß unterziehen.

Fine Waffles (Feine Waffeln)

Ingredients:

Metric		Imperial	
6	eggs, seperated	6	eggs, seperated
300 g	margarine	12 oz	margarine
1/2 t	vanilla extract	1/2 t	vanilla extract
1 pinch	cinnamon	1 pinch	cinnamon
375 ml	milk	3/4 pint	milk
130 g	flour	5 oz	flour
4 t	baking powder	4 t	baking powder

Method:

Beat egg whites until stiff. Cream remaining ingredients in a large bowl to a smooth batter.
Fold in stiffly beaten egg whites. Bake waffles in a hot waffle iron as usual.

Krübbelchen

Zutaten:
- 250 g Quark
- 4 Eier
- 100 g Zucker
- 2 P. Vanillezucker
- 250 g Mehl
- 2 Teel. Backpulver

Zubereitung:
Alle Zutaten zu einem Teig verarbeiten, zu Kugeln formen, und in heißem Öl ausbacken.

Curd Doughnuts (Krübbelchen)

Ingredients:

Metric		Imperial	
250 g	curd	1/2 lb	curd
4	eggs	4	eggs
100 g	sugar	4 oz	sugar
1 t	vanilla extract	1 t	vanilla extract
250 g	flour	1/2 lb	flour
2 t	baking powder	2 t	baking powder

Method:

Mix well all ingredients to a smooth dough. Form balls and deep fry in hot oil. Drain on absorbent kitchen paper before serving.

Fastnachts-Krapfen

Zutaten:

3		Eier
125	g	Butter o. Margar.
1	P.	Vanillezucker
1	Pr.	Salz
125	g	Zucker
500	g	Mehl
1	P.	Hefe

Zubereitung:

Hefe mit etwas warmer Milch und Zucker auflösen und aus den restlichen Zutaten einen Hefeteig bereiten und gehen lassen. Bällchen formen und nochmals gehen lassen, in heißem Fett ausbacken und sofort in Zucker wenden.

Carnaval Doughnuts (Fastnachts-Krapfen)

Ingredients:

Metric		Imperial	
3	eggs	3	eggs
125 g	butter or margarine	5 oz	butter or margarine
1/2 t	vanilla extract	1/2 t	vanilla extract
1 pinch	salt	1 pinch	salt
125 g	sugar	5 oz	sugar
500 g	flour	1 lb	flour
1 packet	dried yeast	1 packet	dried yeast

Method:

Dissolve some sugar in hand hot milk and add yeast. Leave for some minutes until frothy. Mix rest of ingredients. Add yeast mixture and beat well. Let rise in a covered bowl until dough has doubled in size (about 1 hour). Form balls and let rise again. Deep fry in hot oil. When done, drain on an absorbent kitchen paper and immediately turn in sugar.

Badische Scherben

Zutaten:
- 400 g Mehl
- 2 Eier
- 1 Eigelb
- 75 g Butter oder Margarine
- 1/8 ℓ Weißwein oder Rum, Weinbrand
- Backfett
- Zucker
- Zimt

Zubereitung:
Die Eier und das Eigelb mit dem Handrührgerät gut verrühren, das zerlassene lauwarme Fett untermischen, Spirituosen zufügen und zuletzt das gesiebte Mehl gut unterkneten. Teig 1 Stunde kalt stellen, danach zu Rollen formen, in walnußgroße Stücke schneiden und diese auf gut bemehltem Brett sehr dünn auswellen.

Fried "Fragments" (Badische Scherben)

Ingredients:

Metric		Imperial	
400 g	flour	16 oz	flour
2	eggs	2	eggs
1	egg yolk	1	egg yolk
75 g	butter or margarine	3 oz	butter or margarine
125 ml	white wine or rum	1/4 pint	white wine or rum
	cognac		cognac
	oil for deep frying		oil for deep frying
	sugar		sugar
	cinnamon		cinnamon

Method:

Beat eggs and egg yolk until creamy. Melt butter and leave to cool. Add luke-warm butter to egg mixture. Add liquids. Finally add sifted flour. Knead in well. Leave dough in a cool place for one hour. Cut dough in portions and make long rolls. Cut rolls in walnut-sized pieces. Roll out each piece on a floured board until very thin.

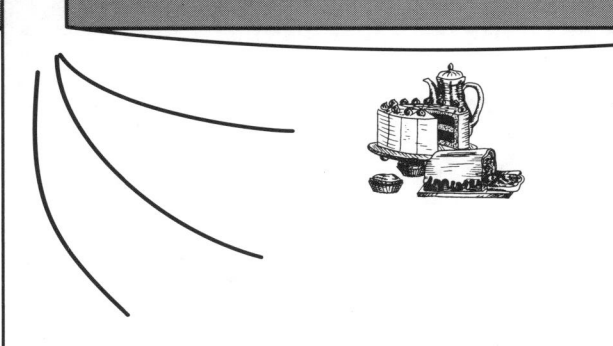

Die Teigblätter in heißem Fett schwimmend ausbacken. Damit sie wellig werden, zwei bis drei Scheiben zugleich ausbacken. Herausnehmen, auf Serviette abtropfen lassen, noch heiß mit etwas Zucker und Zimt bestreuen.

Deep fry two to three "fragments" at the same time so that they turn out crinkly. Drain on absorbent kitchen paper and sprinkle with sugar and cinnamon while still hot.

Berliner Brot

Zutaten:

500	g	Zucker
4		Eier
500	g	ungeschälte süße Mandeln
40	g	ger. Schokolade
5	g	Nelkenpfeffer
5	g	Zimt
500	g	Mehl
1	Msp.	Hirschhornsalz

Zubereitung:

Alle Zutaten zu einem festen Teig verarbeiten, dick ausrollen auf einem heißen Backblech, abbacken und noch warm in Stangen schneiden.

Berlin Bread (Berliner Brot)

Ingredients:

Metric		Imperial	
500 g	sugar	1 lb	sugar
4	eggs	4	eggs
500 g	grated almonds	1 lb	grated almonds
40 g	grated chocolate	1 1/2 oz	grated chocolate
5 g	ground cloves	1 t	ground cloves
5 g	cinnamon	1 t	cinnamon
500 g	flour	1 lb	flour
1/3 t	salt of hartshorn	1/3 t	salt of hartshorn

Method:

Mix well all ingredients to a thick dough. Heat a rectangular baking tray in oven. Roll out dough on hot baking tin. Bake in preheated oven at 175°C/350°F for about 25 minutes. Cut in strips while still warm.

Kalte Hundeschnauze

Zutaten:
- 2 Eier
- 2 Tassen Zucker
- 1 Tasse Kakao
- 1 Eßl. Kaffeepulver
- 250 g geschmolzenes Palmin
- ca. 20 Kekse

Zubereitung:
Eier, Zucker schaumig rühren. Kakao und Kaffeepulver langsam dazu geben. Dann wird das geschmolzene Palmin (nicht zu heiß) untergerührt.
Abwechselnd Schokoladenmasse und Kekse in eine mit Pergamentpapier ausgelegte Kastenform füllen. Über Nacht erkalten lassen, stürzen und in fingerdicke Scheiben schneiden.

Cold Dog's Muzzle (Kalte Hundeschnauze)

Ingredients:

Metric		Imperial	
2	eggs	2	eggs
2 cups	sugar	2 cups	sugar
1 cup	cocoa	1 cup	cocoa
1 T	instant granulated coffee	1 T	instant granulated coffee
250 g	melted palm butter about 20 biscuits	1/2 lb	melted palm butter about 20 biscuits

Method:

Beat eggs and sugar until light and creamy. Add cocoa and instant coffee. Blend in well. Gradually add melted (but not hot) palm butter while stirring continually. Cover a loaf tin with grease proof paper. Put biscuits and batter in tin in alternating layers. Chill over night. Remove from tin and cut in slices.

Nürnberger Elisen-Lebkuchen

Zutaten:

2		Eier
200	g	Zucker
1	P.	Vanillezucker
1	Msp.	gem. Nelken
1	Msp.	Backpulver
1	Tl.	gem. Zimt
½	Fl.	Rum-Aroma
1-2	Tr.	Zitronen-Backöl
75	g	Orangeat
75	g	Zitronat
125	g	gem. Mandeln
125	g	Haselnüsse

Zubereitung:

Man schlägt die Eier schaumig und gibt Zucker und Vanillezucker nach und nach zu, bis eine dicke cremartige Masse entstanden ist. Dann Gewürze und Backpulver zugeben. Teig mit 1 Teel. als kleine Häufchen auf Oblaten setzen. Auf ein ungefettetes Blech geben

Nürnberg Elise Gingerbread
(Nürnberger Elisen-Lebkuchen)

Ingredients:

Metric		Imperial	
2	eggs	2	eggs
200 g	sugar	8 oz	sugar
1/2 t	vanilla extract	1/2 t	vanilla extract
1/3 t	ground cloves	1/3 t	ground cloves
1/3 t	baking powder	1/3 t	baking powder
1 t	cinnamon	1 t	cinnamon
1 T	rum	1 T	rum
1 T	lemon juice	1 T	lemon juice
75 g	candied orange peel	3 oz	candied orange peel
75 g	candied lemon peel	3 oz	candied lemon peel
125 g	grated almonds	5 oz	grated almonds
125 g	grated hazelnuts	5 oz	grated hazelnuts

Method:

Beat eggs until light and creamy. Gradually add sugar and vanilla extract. Continue beating until mixture thickens to a cream. Add spices and baking powder. Using a teaspoon put batter in walnut-size portions on a rectangular baking tray.

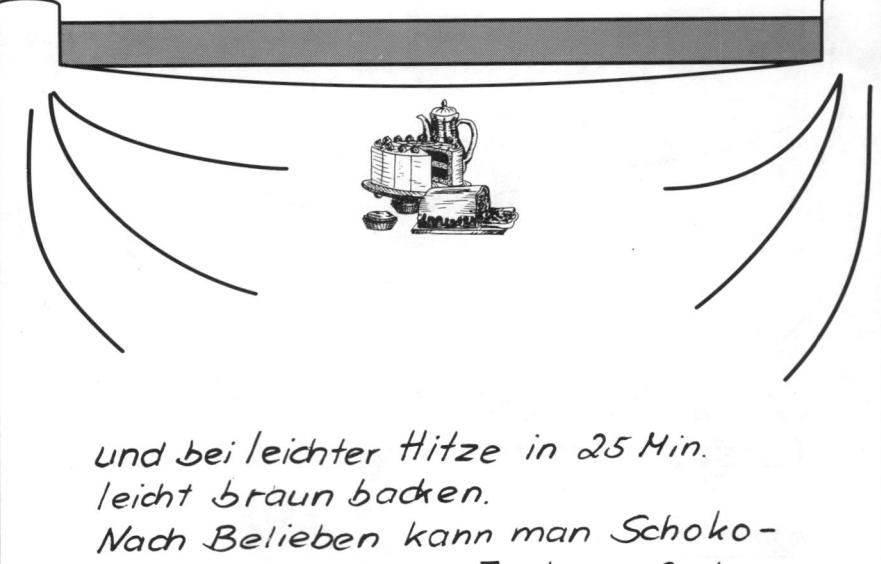

und bei leichter Hitze in 25 Min.
leicht braun backen.
Nach Belieben kann man Schoko-
laden- oder hellen Zuckerguß darübergeben.
Die Lebkuchen schmecken aber
auch ohne Guß sehr gut.

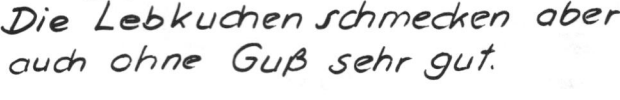

Bake in preheated oven at moderate heat for 25 minutes until light brown. Spread with chocolate or frosting of your choice (optional). The ginger bread is just as tasty without frosting.

Spitzbuben

Zutaten:
- 125 g Fett
- 125 g Zucker
- 20 g Kakao
- 1 P. Vanillezucker
- etwas Zimt
- 125 g ger. Mandeln
- 125 g Mehl
- 1 Teel. Backpulver

Zubereitung:
Fett, Zucker und Kakao schaumig rühren. Gewürze und Mehl mit Backpulver vermischt unterkneten. Teig zum Ruhen kalt stellen. Dann formt man gleichmäßige Kugeln, bestreicht sie mit Eigelb und verziert sie mit einer halbierten Mandel.
Bei schwacher Hitze ca. 15-20 Min. abbacken.

Rascals (Spitzbuben)

Ingredients:

Metric		Imperial	
125 g	shortening	5 oz	shortening
125 g	sugar	5 oz	sugar
20 g	cocoa	1 oz	cocoa
1/2 t	vanilla extract	1/2 t	vanilla extract
	some cinnamon		some cinnamon
125 g	grated almonds	5 oz	grated almonds
125 g	flour	5 oz	flour
1 t	baking powder	1 t	baking powder

Method:

Cream shortening, sugar and cocoa. Add spices. Blend in sifted flour and baking powder. Gradually add to egg mixture while stirring continually. Chill for 1 hour, form not too large balls, all similar in size. Spread with beaten egg yolk and decorate with half an almond.
Bake in preheated oven at a moderate heat for 15-20 minutes.

Kolatschen

Zutaten:
- 125 g Butter
- 70 g Zucker
- 1 Eigelb
- 1 P. Vanillezucker
- 200-220 g Mehl
- 1 Teel. Backpulver
- Marmelade zum Füllen

Zubereitung:
Einen Knetteig bereiten und zu walnußgroßen Kugeln formen, in Eiweiß und Hagelzucker tauchen, mit einem Löffelstiel eine Vertiefung in die Mitte drücken und mit Marmelade füllen. Bei mittlerer Hitze backen.

Filled Oven-baked Doughnuts (Kolatschen)

Ingredients:

Metric		Imperial	
dough:			
125 g	butter	5 oz	butter
70 g	sugar	3 oz	sugar
1	egg yolk	1	egg yolk
200-220 g	flour	8-11 oz	flour
1/2 t	vanilla extract	1/2 t	vanilla extract
1 t	baking powder	1 t	baking powder
dip:			
1	egg white	1	egg white
	nib-sugar		nib-sugar
	jam for filling		jam for filling

Method:

Mix all dough ingredients to a smooth dough. Form walnut sized balls. Dip in egg white and nib-sugar. Using the round end of a wooden spoon, press a hole in each ball. Fill with jam. Bake in pre-heated oven at moderate heat until light brown.

Nougat - Kipferln

Zutaten:
- 100 g Butter
- 200 g Nougatmasse
- 1 Ei
- 1 P. Vanillezucker
- 1 Messersp. Salz
- 300 g Mehl
- 1/2 Teel. Backpulver

Zubereitung:

Alle Zutaten der Reihe nach in einen Knetteig verarbeiten. Eine Stunde kühl stellen, dann eine Rolle formen, davon gleich große Stücke schneiden und Kipferl formen ∩. Auf einem Backblech im vorgeheizten Ofen bei 180° hellbraun backen.

Erkaltete Kipferl kann man an den Spitzen mit Schokoladenglasur bestreichen.

Nougat Crescent Rolls (Nougat-Kipferln)

Ingredients:

Metric		Imperial	
100 g	butter	4 oz	butter
200 g	nougat	8 oz	nougat
1	egg	1	egg
1/2 t	vanilla extract	1/2 t	vanilla extract
1 small pinch of salt		1 small pinch of salt	
300 g	flour	12 oz	flour
1/2 t	baking powder	1/2 t	baking powder

Method:

Beat butter to a cream. Add nougat. Add egg and flavouring. Beat until light and creamy. Gradually add sifted flour and baking powder. Beat to a smooth dough. Chill for one hour. Portion dough to make long rolls. Cut in smaller pieces and form small crescent rolls (2x4 cm/1x1 1/2 inches).

Bake in preheated oven at 180°C/350°F until light brown. When crescents are cold, dip the edges of the crescents in chocolate glaze.

Salzbrezeln

Zutaten:
- 500 g Mehl
- 25 g Hefe
- 40 g Zucker
- 75 g Schweineschmalz
- 1/4 l Milch
- 1 Teel. Salz

Zubereitung:

Aus den Zutaten einen Hefeteig bereiten und 30 Min. gehen lassen. Dann zu etwa 1 cm dicken Rollen verarbeiten und auf einem gefetteten Blech zu Brezeln formen.
Mit lauwarmem Wasser bestreichen und mit grobem Salz bestreuen.
Brezeln bei 220° ca. 30 Min. abbacken.

Salted Pretzels (Salzbrezeln)

Ingredients:

Metric		Imperial	
500 g	flour	1 lb	flour
25 g	compressed yeast	1 oz	compressed yeast
40 g	sugar	1 1/2 oz	sugar
75 g	lard	3 oz	lard
250 ml	hand-hot milk	1/2 pint	hand-hot milk
1 t	salt	1 t	salt

Method:

Dissolve some sugar in hand-hot milk. Add crumbled yeast, dissolve and leave for a while until frothy. Add to rest of ingredients and knead to a smooth dough. Let rise in a covered bowl for 1 hour or until dough has doubled in size. Portion dough and form 1 cm(1/2) thick rolls. Grease a rectangular baking tray. Form pretzels on the tin. Brush with lukewarm water and sprinkle with coarse salt. Bake in preheated oven at 220°C/400-450°F for about 30 minutes.

**He who entertains the foreigner,
does more for peace in his country
than the strongest, most courageous
and well-armed soldier.**
                                                    Chinese Proverb

*Wer den Fremden freundlich bewirtet,
der leistet mehr für den Frieden im Lande
als der stärkste Soldat
mit den besten Waffen
und mit dem größten Mut.*
                                                    aus China

Holiday Favorites

(Was uns im Urlaub gut schmeckte)

Oberpfälzer Hollerkoch

Zutaten:
- 500 g Holunderbeeren
- 2-3 schöne, reife Birnen
- 1 süß-saurer Apfel
- 125 g reife Pflaumen
- Zucker
- Zimt, Vanille
- Mehl od. Speisestärke

Zubereitung:

Stengel der Holunderbeeren entfernen. Birnen und Äpfel schälen und in Stücke schneiden. Pflaumen entsteinen und vierteln. Alle Früchte vermischen und mit Zucker bestreuen, durchziehen lassen, dann unter Rühren zum Kochen bringen. Mit Zimt, Zucker und Zitrone abschmecken, mit Mehl oder Stärke binden und nochmal abschmecken. Warm oder kalt servieren.

Upper Palatinate Elder-Berry (Oberpfälzer Hollerkoch)

Ingredients:

Metric		Imperial	
500 g	elder-berries	1 lb	elder-berries
2-3	firm pears, peeled, cored and sliced	2-3	firm pears, peeled, cored and sliced
1	sweet-sour apple, peeled, cored and sliced	1	sweet-sour apple, peeled, cored and sliced
125 g	ripe plums, stoned and quartered	5 oz	ripe plums, stoned and quartered
	sugar		sugar
	lemon juice		lemon juice
	cinnamon, vanilla		cinnamon, vanilla
	flour or corn starch		flour or corn starch

Method:

Wash and remove elder-berries from stems. Put all fruits into large saucepan, sprinkle with sugar and leave for a while. Slowly bring to the boil. Stir occassionally. Add, lemon juice, cinnamon and vanilla to taste. Thicken with some flour or corn starch. May be served warm or cold.

Zwiebelkuchen (Schwaben)

Zutaten:

Teig:
- 250 g Mehl
- 15 g Hefe
- 1 Prise Salz
- 1 Ei
- 1 Eßl. Öl
- 1/8 l Milch

Füllung:
- 100 g Butter od. Marg.
- 5 Eßl. Mehl
- 5 Eßl. Milch
- 4 Eier
- 1 kg Zwiebeln
- magerer Speck
- Pfeffer, Salz, Maggi

Zubereitung:

Aus den angegebenen Zutaten einen Hefeteig bereiten, in einer Springform ausrollen und einen Rand andrücken.

Füllung bereiten: Butter zergehen

Onion Pie / Swabia (Zwiebelkuchen / Schwaben)

Ingredients:

Metric		Imperial	
Dough:			
250 g	plain flour	10 oz	plain flour
15 g	compressed yeast	1/2 oz	compressed yeast
1 pinch	salt	1 pinch	salt
1	egg	1	egg
1 T	cooking oil	1 T	cooking oil
125 ml	hand-hot milk	1/4 pint	hand-hot milk
Filling:			
100 g	butter or margarine	4 oz	butter or margarine
5 T	flour	5 T	flour
4	eggs	4	eggs
1 kg	onions, peeled and sliced	2 lbs	onions, peeled anmd sliced
	lean bacon, diced		lean bacon, diced
salt, pepper, liquid seasoning		salt, pepper, liquid seasoning	

Method:

Make a smooth dough as usual. Leave in a warm place until dough has reached double its bulk (30 minutes). Melt butter, stir in flour. Gradually add milk, constantly stirring. Add eggs and continue whisking.

lassen, Mehl einrühren, Milch unterrühren und Eier einquirlen; Zwiebeln in Ringe schneiden, mageren Speck in Würfel schneiden und beides in der Pfanne dünsten, abgekühlt in die angerührten Zutaten geben, mit Salz, Pfeffer und Maggi abschmecken.

Zwiebelmasse auf den Teig geben und bei 175° etwa 1 Std. backen.

Remove from heat. Add seasoning, braised onions and bacon. Line baking tray with dough. Pour on onion mixture.
Bake in preheated oven at 175° C (350° F) for approx. 1 hour.

Schwarzwälder Schäufele

Zutaten (8-10 Portionen)

etwa	1,5 kg	gepökelte, leicht geräucherte Schweineschulter
etwa	3 L	Wasser
	1	Zwiebel
	6	Nelken
	1 Teel.	weiße Pfefferkörner
	1 Teel.	Wacholderbeeren
	½ Teel.	Thymian
	1	Lorbeerblatt

Zubereitung:

Die Schweineschulter in heißem Wasser abspülen. Wasser in einem passenden Topf aufsetzen, zerschnittene Zwiebel, Nelken, Pfefferkörner, Wacholderbeeren, Thymian und Lorbeerblatt zufügen und aufkochen, das Fleisch hineinlegen und etwa 10 Min. kochen lassen. Bei schwacher Hitze noch etwa 1½ Std. zugedeckt ziehen lassen.

Black Forest Shovel (Schwarzwälder Schäufele)

Ingredients (8-10 portions):

Metric		Imperial	
1 1/2 kg	cured shoulder of pork	3 lb	cured shoulder of pork
3 l	water	6 pints	water
1	onion, peeled and sliced	1	onion, peeled and sliced
6	cloves	6	cloves
1 t	white peppercorns	1 t	white peppercorns
1 t	juniper berries	1 t	juniper berries
1/2 t	thyme	1/2 t	thyme
1	bay leaf	1	bay leaf

Method:

Wash and clean meat. Put water, onions and spices in a large cooking pot. Bring to the boil, add meat. Boil for about 10 minutes. Turn down heat, place lid on pot and simmer for another 1 1/2 hours. Remove meat from pot and slice.

Das Fleisch aus der Brühe nehmen und aufschneiden. Mit Mixed Pickles, Senf und Bauernbrot zu Kartoffelsalat servieren.
Dazu ein kühles Bier kredenzen.

Dieses Gericht macht wenig Arbeit und ist ein beliebtes Gästeessen.

Tip: Eventuelle Reste kalt aufschneiden und zum Abendbrot anbieten!

Serve with mixed pickles, mustard and rye bread or potato salad. Beverage: a cool beer.

This meal is easy to prepare and will be loved by your guests. Leftovers may be served cold.

Allgäuer Käs-Spätzle

Zutaten:
- 250 g Mehl
- 2 Eier
- 1 starke Prise Salz
- ca. 1/8 l Wasser (je nach Bedarf)
- Speck od. Butter
- Emmentaler Käse

Zubereitung:

Mehl, Salz und Eier verrühren und nur schluckweise Wasser zugeben, kräftig schlagen bis der zähe Teig blasig ist. Mit einer Spätzlereibe in kochendes Salzwasser hineinreiben. Man kann den Teig auch durch eine andere grobe Reibe streichen.

Speck auslassen oder Butter bräunen, Spätzle hineingeben. Käse darüberreiben. Dazu schmeckt grüner Salat oder Tomatensalat.

German Cheese Noodles (Allgäuer Käs-Spätzle)

Ingredients:

Metric		Imperial	
250 g	plain flour	1/2 lb	plain flour
2	eggs	2	eggs
1 large pinch salt		1 large pinch salt	
approx. 125 ml water		approx. 1/4 pint water	
	chopped bacon or butter		chopped bacon or butter
	grated Swiss cheese		grated Swiss cheese

Method:

Beat flour, eggs, salt, whilst gradually adding water until light and smooth.

Bring lightly salted water to the boil in a large cooking pot. Turn down heat. Add some butter or margarine. Turn out some dough on to a board. Scape off bits of dough with a sharp knife into boiling water. Noodles are done when they surface. Remove from water with a skimmer and rinse in cold water. Repeat procedure with rest of dough.

Fry chopped bacon or heat butter, stir in noodles and sprinkle with grated cheese.

Serve hot with lettuce or tomato salad.

Kaiserschmarrn (Österreich)

Zutaten:
- 125 g Mehl
- 1/4 l Milch
- 4 Eier, getrennt
- 2 P. Vanillezucker
- 1 Prise Salz
- Butter od. Marg. z. Braten

Zubereitung:

Mehl, Milch, Eigelb, Vanillinzucker und Salz zu einem glatten Teig verrühren. Eiweiß steif schlagen und darunterziehen. Fett in einer Pfanne erhitzen und 1/3 des Teiges hineingeben. Unterseite goldbraun backen, wenden, Teig kurz stocken lassen, mit zwei Gabeln in Stücke reißen und rundum bräunen. Mit dem restlichen Teig ebenso verfahren.

Emperors Broken Pancake / Austria (Kaiserschmarrn / Österreich)

Ingredients:

Metric		Imperial	
125 g	plain flour	5 oz	plain flour
250 ml	milk	1/2 pint	milk
4	eggs, separated	4	eggs, separated
1 t	vanilla extract	1 t	vanilla extract
1 pinch	salt	1 pinch	salt
butter or margarine for frying		butter or margarine for frying	

Method:

Whisk flour, milk, egg yolks, vanilla extract and salt to a smooth batter. Whisk egg whites until fluffy. Fold into batter.
Heat butter or margarine in a pan. Pour in 1/3 of batter. Fry over moderate heat until underside is golden. Flip pancake carefully. Using two forks, tear pancake into pieces. Turn out into warmed dish, and sprinkle with sugar. Repeat procedure with rest of batter. Serve hot.

Dampfnudeln (Elsaß)

Zutaten:
- 500 g Mehl
- 50 g Zucker
- 30 g Hefe
- 1/4 l Milch
- 1 Ei
- 50 g Butter
- Zitronenaroma
- 1 Prise Salz

zum Dämpfen:
- 1/4 l Milch
- 40 g Butter
- 50 g Zucker
- 1 Prise Salz

zur Soße:
- 1/2 l Weißwein
- etwas Stärkemehl
- Zucker
- 1 Eigelb

Zubereitung:

Aus den angegeben Zutaten einen Hefeteig bereiten und gehen lassen. Etwa 4-5 Klöße formen und in eine Auflaufform legen, gehen lassen. Die leicht erwärmte Milch mit

Steamed Dumplings / Alsace (Dampfnudeln / Elsaß)

Ingredients:

Metric		Imperial	

Dumplings:
500 g	plain flour	1 lb	plain flour
50 g	sugar	2 oz	sugar
30 g	compressed yeast	1 oz	compressed yeast
250 ml	milk	1/2 pint	milk
1	egg	1	egg
50 g	butter	2 oz	butter
	lemon juice		lemon juice
1 pinch	salt	1 pinch	salt

For steaming:
250 ml	milk	1/2 pint	milk
40 g	butter	2 oz	butter
50 g	sugar	2 oz	sugar
1 pinch	salt	1 pinch	salt

For sauce:
500 ml	white wine	1 pint	white wine
	corn starch		corn starch
	sugar		sugar
1	egg yolk	1	egg yolk

den Zutaten zum Dämpfen darübergeben und bei ca. 200° auf der unteren Schiene im Backofen etwa 50 Min. garen.

Weinsoße bereiten: Wein aufkochen und mit Speisestärke binden, mit Zucker und Zitronensaft abschmecken. Eigelb einquirlen, nicht mehr kochen.

Weinsoße heiß zu den heißen Dampfnudeln servieren.

Method:

Dumplings:
Dissolve 1 level teaspoon sugar in lukewarm milk in small basin. Add crumbled yeast and stir until dissolved. Cover and leave in a warm place for about 10 minutes. Melt butter and let cool. Mix flour and sugar in a bowl. Beat egg and salt. Beat all ingredients briskly to a smooth dough. Leave to rise for about 1 hour or until dough has doubled its bulk. Form 4-5 dumplings, put in a pie dish and leave to rise again.

Heat milk and other steaming ingredients. Do not boil. Pour over dumplings and cook on the lowest shelf of a preheated oven at 200° C (400° F) for about 50 minutes.

For sauce:
Put corn starch in a small bowl, add some tablespoons of wine and blend to a paste. Bring wine to the boil, whisk in paste until sauce thickens. Blend in lemon juice and sugar to taste. Remove from heat. Briskly whisk in egg yolk. Serve hot with dumplings.

Coq au vin – Hahn in Rotwein
(Frankreich)

Zutaten:
- 1 große Poularde (~1200 g)
- 30 g Butter
- 2-3 Eßl. Olivenöl
- 125 g mageren Speck
- 3 mittl. Zwiebeln
- 1 Gläschen Cognac
- 1 Glas Champignon
- 1/2 Flasche Burgunder-Rotwein
- Salz, Pfeffer, Thymian
- 2 Lorbeerblätter
- 1 Knoblauchzehe
- Mehl oder Soßenbinder

Zubereitung:

In einem Bräter oder einer Kasserolle Speck mit Butter und Öl anbraten, gehackte Zwiebeln dazugeben, tranchiertes Hähnchen hineingeben und goldbraun anbraten, würzen und mit Cognac flambieren (wichtig!), halbierte Champignons, Lorbeer, Thymian und zerhackten Knoblauch dazu-

Chicken in Red Wine / France
(Coq au vin - Hahn in Rotwein / Frankreich)

Ingredients:

Metric	Imperial
1 large chicken (1200 g) cleaned and cut into portions	1 large chicken (2 1/2 lb) cleaned and cut into portions
30 g butter	1 oz butter
2-3 T olive oil	2-3 T olive oil
125 g diced lean bacon	5 oz diced lean bacon
3 medium-sized onions, peeled/chopped	3 medium-sized onions, peeled/chopped
1 liqueur glass cognac	1 liqueur glass cognac
1 jar mushrooms, drained and halved	1 jar mushrooms, drained and halved
1/2 bottle Burgundy (French Red Wine)	1/2 bottle Burgundy (French Red Wine)
salt, pepper, thyme	salt, pepper, thyme
2 bay leaves	2 bay leaves
1 clove garlic, crushed	1 clove garlic, crushed
flour or corn starch	flour or corn starch

geben, zum Schluß den Rotwein
hineingeben und alles 20. Min.
dünsten lassen. Evtl. mit Mehl
oder Soßenbinder abbinden.
In der Kasserolle servieren.

Als Tischwein reicht man dazu:
        Burgunder, Côte au Rhone

Method:

Heat butter and olive oil in a casserole. Braise bacon, onions until transparent, add chicken pieces and fry until golden brown. Season with salt and pepper. Pour over cognac and set alight (important!).

Add mushrooms, bay leaves, thyme, crushed garlic and finally, the red wine. Simmer over moderate heat for 20 minutes or until chicken is done. Remove chicken from casserole and thicken sauce with corn starch or flour (optional). Return chicken to casserole and reheat. Serve with French red wine (Burgundy).

Apfelkuchen (England)

Zutaten:
- 200 g Zucker
- 1 P. Vanillinzucker
- 3 Eier
- 1 Zitrone (Saft u. Schale)
- 300 g Mehl
- 1/2 P. Backpulver
- 750 g säuerl. Äpfel

Zubereitung:

Aus den Zutaten einen Rührteig bereiten. Äpfel in Würfel schneiden und unter den Teig heben und in eine gefettete Kastenform füllen. Im vorgeheizten Backofen bei 175° auf der unteren Schiene ca. 40-45 Min. backen.

Diesen Kuchen serviert man heiß oder kalt mit Vanillesoße.

Apple Cake / England
(Apfelkuchen / England)

Ingredients:

Metric		Imperial	
200 g	sugar	8 oz	sugar
1/2 t	vanilla extract	1/2 t	vanilla extract
3	eggs	3	eggs
grated rind and juice of one untreated lemon		grated rind and juice of one untreated lemon	
300 g	plain flour	12 oz	plain flour
2 t	baking powder	2 t	baking powder
750 g	sour apples, peeled, cored, diced	1 1/2 lbs	sour apples, peeled, cored, diced1

Method:

Cream sugar, vanilla, eggs and lemon. Blend in sifted flour and baking powder. Beat briskly.

Fold in diced apple and pour into greased loaf tin. Bake in a preheated oven at 175° C (350° F) for about 40-45 minutes, or until skewer, inserted into the centre of cake, comes out clean.

Serve hot or cold with custard or vanilla sauce.

Leberpastete (Dänemark)

Zutaten:
- 280 g Leber
- 250 g Speck
- 50 g Margarine
- 50 g Mehl
- ca. 1/2 l Milch
- Pfeffer, Salz
- Zwiebeln und Kräuter n. Geschm.

Zubereitung:

Leber und Speck durch den Fleischwolf geben, Zwiebeln und Kräuter hacken, alle Zutaten gut vermischen. In eine mit Alufolie ausgelegte Kastenform geben und ca. 1 Std. bei 190-200° auf mittlerer Schiene backen.

Live Pâté / Denmark
(Leberpastete / Dänemark)

Ingredients:

Metric		Imperial	
280 g	liver	11 oz	liver
250 g	bacon	10 oz	bacon
50 g	margarine	2 oz	margarine
50 g	flour	2 oz	flour
500 ml	milk	1 pint	milk
salt, pepper, onions, herbs		salt, pepper, onions, herbs	

Method:
Clean and mince liver and bacon. Clean and chop onions and herbs. Add salt and pepper, margarine, milk and flour. Mix all ingredients well. Put mixture in a greased rectangular baking tin, cover with aluminium foil. Bake in preheated oven at 190° - 200° C (375° - 400° F) for about an hour.

Hefeschnecken (Dänemark)

Zutaten:
- 250 g geschmolzene Margarine
- 1 Tasse warme Milch
- 4 geschlagene Eier
- 1 P. Hefe
- 4 Eßl. Zucker
- 1-2 Msp. Kardamon
- ca. 500 g Mehl (Menge nach Bedarf)
- Rosinen
- Zimt

Zubereitung:

Aus den Zutaten einen Hefeteig bereiten und gut gehen lassen. Teig ausrollen, mit Rosinen und Zimt bestreuen, eine Rolle daraus machen und in Scheiben schneiden. Scheiben auf ein Blech legen und gehen lassen. 20 Min. bei 215°C abbacken.

Danish Rolled Buns (Hefeschnecken / Dänemark)

Ingredients:

Metric		Imperial	
250 g	butter or margarine, melted	10 oz	butter or margarine, melted
1 cup	luke-warm water	1 cup	luke-warm water
4	beaten eggs	4	beaten eggs
1 cake	compressed yeast	1 cake	compressed yeast
4 T	sugar	4 T	sugar
2 pinch	cardamom	2 pinch	cardamom
500 g	plain flour	1 lb	plain flour
	raisins, cinnamon		raisins, cinnamon

Method:

Dissolve level teaspoon sugar and some milk in a small bowl. Crumble yeast and dissolve. Cover and leave until frothy. Mix well rest of milk, sugar, spices and beaten eggs. Fold in 1 cup flour.

Gradually add remaining flour, kneading continually, to make a smooth, but not too thick dough. Cover mixing bowl and leave dough to rise in a warm place until double in bulk. Knead again and roll out to a large 1/2 cm (1/4 inch) thick rectangle. Sprinkle with cinnamon and spread over raisins. Roll the rectangle together. Cut roll into 1 1/2 cm (1/2 inch) thick slices. Put slices onto greased baking tray and let rise. Bake in preheated oven at $215°-220°$ C ($400°-425°$ F) until golden brown.

Grobe Weizenbrötchen

(Dänische Boller)

Zutaten:
- 50 g Hefe
- 400 ccm Lauwarmes Wasser
- 1 Eßl. Salz
- 1 Eßl. Öl
- 70 g Grahammehl
- 70 g Vollkornweizenmehl
- 550 g Weizenmehl

Zubereitung:

Hefe im Wasser auflösen und mit den übrigen Zutaten gut verkneten, an warmer Stelle ca. 30 Min. gehen lassen. Aus dem Teig ca. 18 kleine Brötchen formen und auf einem gefetteten Blech nochmal 20 Min. gehen lassen, einschneiden und im vorgeheizten Ofen bei 250° abbacken. Ei mit Wasser verquirlen u. die Brötchen damit einpinseln.

Whole Wheat Rolls / Danish "Boller"
(Grobe Weizenbrötchen / Dänische Boller)

Ingredients:

Metric		Imperial	
50 g	compressed yeast	2 oz	compressed yeast
400 ml	luke-warm water	16 fl oz	luke-warm water
1 T	salt	1 T	salt
1 T	oil	1 T	oil
70 g	Grahan flour	3 oz	Graham flour
70 g	course wholemeal	3 oz	course wholemeal
550 g	wheaten flour	1 lb 2 oz	wheaten flour

Method:

Dissolve yeast in some water. Mix dry ingredients in a large bowl, form a well. Pour in dissolved yeast and beat briskly, slowly adding remaining water and oil. Knead well (10-12 min). Cover bowl and leave dough to rise until double in bulk. Knead once again. Form 18 rolls and put on greased baking tray. Leave to rise for another 20 minutes. Cut across tops with a sharp knife. Beat egg and water in a cup and paint rolls. Bake in preheated oven at 250° C (500° F) for 30 - 40 min.

Jugoslawischer Mussaka

Zutaten:

- 800 g Auberginen
- 500 g Zuccini
- Saft von 1 Zitrone
- 4-6 Eßl. Mehl
- 1/4 L Öl
- 1 Zwiebel
- 1 Knoblauchzehe
- 600 g gemischtes Hack
- Kräuter
- Tomatenmark
- 4 Eier
- 0,2 L saure Sahne
- 2 Eßl. geriebenen Käse

Zubereitung:

Auberginen und Zuccini in 2cm-dicke Scheiben schneiden und 30 Min. mit Zitronensaft ziehen lassen. Scheiben abtropfen, in Mehl wenden und in Öl von beiden Seiten goldbraun anbraten. Hackfleisch mit geschnittener Zwiebel und zerdrückter Knoblauch-

Yugoslavian Moussaka
(Jugoslawischer Mussaka)

Ingredients:

Metric		Imperial	
800 g	aubergines, washed and sliced	1 1/2 lbs	aubergines, washed and sliced
500 g	courgettes, washed and sliced	1 lb	courgettes, washed and sliced
	juice of one lemon		juice of one lemon
4-6 T	flour	4-6 T	flour
250 ml	oil (olive oil)	1/2 pint	oil (olive oil)
1	onion, peeled and chopped	1	onion, peeled and chopped
1 clove	garlic, peeled and crushed	1 clove	garlic, peeled and crushed
300 g	minced pork	12 oz	minced pork
300 g	minced beef	12 oz	minced beef
	tomato purée		tomato purée
4	eggs	4	eggs
200 ml	soured cream	6-8 fl oz	soured cream
2 T	grated cheese	2 T	grated cheese
	salt, pepper		salt, pepper

Method:
Sprinkle aubergine and courgette slices with lemon juice and leave to marinate for about 30 minutes.

zehe leicht anbraten und würzen. Auberginen, Hack und Zuccini in eine feuerfeste Form schichten. Die oberste Schicht muß Gemüse sein. Eier mit saurer Sahne, Käse und Pfeffer verquirlen und über den Auflauf geben. 50 Min. bei 200-250° im Ofen backen.

Dazu reicht man Reis und Salat.

Drain slices and dust with flour. Fry in hot oil on both sides to a golden brown. Drain on absorbent paper. Braise meat, onion and garlic in hot oil until golden. Season. Put meat, aubergines and courgettes in alternating layers in a shallow ovenproof dish. The top layer should be vegetable. Whisk eggs, soured cream, pepper and cheese. Pour over meat and vegetables. Bake at 200°-250° C (400°- 500° F) for 50 minutes. Serve with rice, and lettuce or tomato salad.

Güvetsch (Jugoslawien)

Zutaten:
- 100 g Räucherspeck
- 4 EßL. Öl
- 4 Zwiebeln
- 2 Knoblauchzehen
- 500 g gemischtes Hack
- Tomaten
- Paprikaschoten
- grüne Bohnen
- Salatgurke
- Salz
- Paprika
- Thymian
- Bohnenkraut
- Petersilie

Zubereitung:

Speck würfeln und leicht rösten, Öl dazugeben, Zwiebeln und Knoblauch darin goldgelb dünsten. Hack salzen und pfeffern, dazugeben und anbraten. Nacheinander die geschnittenen Tomaten, Paprikaschoten (streifen), geputzte Bohnen und in Schei-

Güvetsch (Yugoslavia / Jugoslawien)

Ingredients:

Metric		Imperial	
100 g	smoked bacon, diced	4 oz	smoked bacon, diced
4 T	oil	4 T	oil
4	onions	4	onions
2 clvs	garlic, peeled and crushed	2 clvs	garlic, peeled and crushed
250 g	minced pork	1/2 lb	minced pork
250 g	minced beef	1/2 lb	minced beef
	tomatoes, sliced		tomatoes, sliced
sweet peppers, cleaned and sliced		sweet peppers, cleaned and sliced	
green beans, trimmed and sliced		green beans, trimmed and sliced	
1 cucumber, washed and sliced		1 cucumber, washed and sliced	
salt, pepper		salt, pepper	
thyme, savory, parsley		thyme, savory, parsley	

Method:
Fry bacon, onions and garlic in a large pan until transparent. Season minced meat with salt and pepper. Add to bacon and onions.

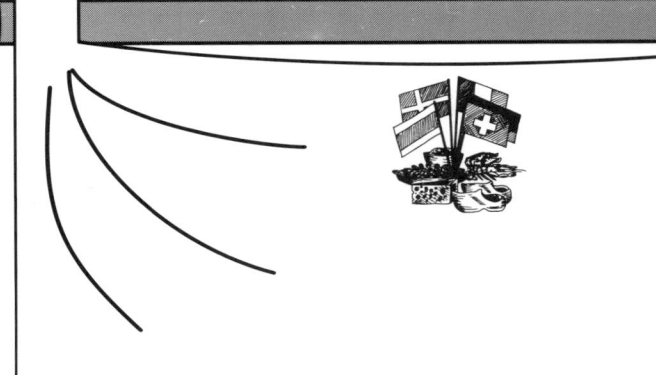

ben geschnittene Gurke darauf schichten, mit etwas Wasser auffüllen und schmoren lassen bis das Gemüse weich ist. Mit den Gewürzen kräftig abschmecken.

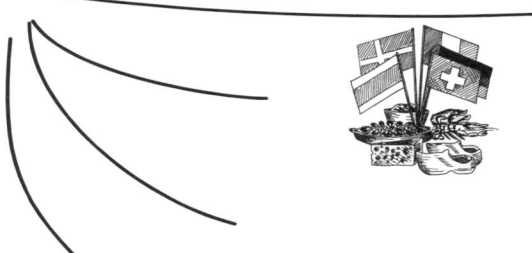

Add tomatoes, peppers, beans and cucumber, in given order. Pour on some water. Let simmer over moderate heat until vegetables are tender. Season well with herbs and spices. Serve with rice.

Contents

(Inhaltsverzeichnis)

Contents
(Inhaltsverzeichnis)

Page / Seite

Prayers of Thanksgiving
(Tischgebete vor dem Essen) 1

According to Backes Rules
(Der Backes und seine Ordnung) 2

Backes' Leavened bread
(Backesbruet) 4

From Grandmas Kitchen

Leaven
(Sauerteig) 5

Grated potato cake
(Sijerlänner Räiwekoche) 6

Apple or plum cake
(Aebbel- / Gwätschekoche) 7

Doughnuts
(Krebbelcher) 8

"Raw" Potato Pancakes
(Räiwekechelcher) 9

Pancakes
(Weisse Kechelcher) 10

"Raw" Potato Waffles
(Geriewene Waffeln) 11

Cooked Potato Waffles
(Waffeln beat gekochde Doffeln) 12

Contents
(Inhaltsverzeichnis)

Page / Seite

Dumplings made of raw potatoes
(Rohe Doffelkliase) 13

Dumplings made from cooked potatoes
(Kliase us gekochde Doffeln) 14

Potato soup
(Breedoffeln) 15

Potato Pancake
(Schdotzkoche) 16

Sliced Potatoes in Cream Sauce
(Gequallte Gestallte) 17

Onion Dip
(Zwiwwelsschdibb) 18

Egg Curd
(Sijerlänner Eierkäs) 19

Buttermilk soup
(Kiernmelchsobbe) 20

Beer soup
(Biersobbe) 21

Plum Jam
(Gwätschekrud) 22

Plums in red wine
(Ruetwänggwätsche) 23

Contents
(Inhaltsverzeichnis)

Page / Seite

Soups and Casseroles

Siegerlaender Shepherds Stew
(Siegerländer Hirtentopf) 24

Autumn casserole
(Herbsteintopf) 26

Pork sausage hotchpotch
(Fleischwurst-Allerlei) 27

Rice dish
(Reistopf) 28

Gaisburger Marsch 29

Brussel Sprouts casserole
(Rosenkohltopf) 30

Sweet pepper casserole
(Paprikaeintopf) 31

Kohlrabi casserole
(Kohlrabitopf) 32

Garnised chicken - stew
(Garniertes Hähnchen - Eintopf) 33

Mushroomsoup
(Champignonsuppe) 34

Cabbage soup
(Krautsuppe) 35

Contents
(Inhaltsverzeichnis)

Page / Seite

Spicy Sauerkraut Soup
(Herzhafte Sauerkrautsuppe) 36

Bread soup with liver-sausage
(Brotsuppe mit Leberwurst) 37

Real Hungarian Goulashsoup
(Echte ungarische Gulaschsuppe) 38

Elder-berry soup
(Holunderbeersuppe) 40

Meat, Poultry and Egg Dishes

Filet - Stroganoff 41

Cured Spare-rib of Pork Kasseler Style
(Kasseler Spezial) 42

Sliced pork in cream sauce
(Geschnetzeltes) 43

Sausage Escalopes
(Bratwurstschnitzel) 45

Onion escalopes
(Zwiebelschnitzel) 46

Goulash with fruit
(Früchtegulasch) 47

Cooked Veal in Dill Sauce
(Gekochtes Kalbfleisch in Dillsoße) 48

Contents
(Inhaltsverzeichnis)

Page / Seite

Hearts of veal in lemon sauce
(Kalbsherz in Zitronensauce) 49

Smoked meat with fruit
(Schlesisches Himmelreich) 51

Farmer's treat
(Bauernschmaus) 52

Minced meat rolls
(Rouladen aus Hackfleisch) 54

Meatballs with Oranges
(Frikadellen mit Orangen) 56

Orangesauce to serve with roast turkey
(Orangensauce zum Putenbraten) 57

Chicken drumstick with lemon
(Hähnchenkeule mit Zitrone) 58

Mimosa eggs
(Mimoseneier) 59

"Lost" eggs on rice
(Verlorene Eier auf Reissockel) 60

Eggs in white sauce
(Überbackene Eier) 61

Contents
(Inhaltsverzeichnis)

Page / Seite

Vegetable and Potato Dishes

Baked brussels sprouts
(Überbackener Rosenkohl) 62

Stuffed cauliflower
(Gefüllter Blumenkohl) 63

Winesauerkraut with grapes
(Weinsauerkraut mit Trauben) 65

Stuffed Cabbage or Savoy
(Gefüllter Kohl) 66

Beans in Tomato Sauce
(Weiße Bohnen in Tomatensauce) 67

Broad Beans with Bacon
(Dicke Bohnen mit Speck) 68

Red Cabbage with Apple
(Rotkohl mit Äpfeln) 69

French Beans with Apple and Tomato
(Brechbohnen mit Äpfeln und Tomaten) 71

Cheese Spinach with Pancakes
(Käsespinat mit Pfannkuchen) 72

French Beans and Tomatoes
(Grüne Bohnen mit Tomaten) 74

Potato Dumplings with Pep
(Kartoffelknödel mit Pfiff) 75

Contents
(Inhaltsverzeichnis)

Page / Seite

Cobblers Casserole
(Schusterpfanne) 76

Casseroles and Soufflés

Curd Soufflé with Apples
(Quarkauflauf mit Äpfeln) 77

Slumbering apple
(Schlummerapfel) 78

Apple-Bread-Pie
(Apfel-Brot-Auflauf) 80

Cherry and Whoemeal Bread Pie
(Kirsch-Schwarzbrot-Auflauf) 82

Spicy Mushroom Pie
(Deftiger Pilzauflauf) 84

Rhubarb-pie
(Rhabarber-Auflauf) 86

Cherry Pie
(Kirschauflauf) 88

Spinach Pie
(Spinat-Auflauf) 89

Plum Potato Pie
(Pflaumen-Kartoffel-Auflauf) 90

Sauerkraut Casserole
(Sauerkrautauflauf) 92

Contents
(Inhaltsverzeichnis)

Page / Seite

Ham and Rice Dish
(Schinkenreis) 94

Red Cabbage in Ring of Baked Fish
(Rotkohl in gebackenem Fischring) 95

Minced Meat and Potato Pie
(Kartoffelauflauf mit Hackfleisch) 96

Swallows' Nests
(Schwalbennester) 98

Cheese and Mushroom Pie
(Champignon-Käse-Torte) 100

Salads

Cheese Salad
(Käsesalat) 102

Cheese and Cold Meat Salad
(Käse-Wurst-Salat) 103

Egg and Cheese Salad
(Käse-Eier-Salat) 104

Rice Salad
(Reissalat) 106

Gentlemans Salad
(Herrensalat) 107

Vegetable Salad
(Gemüsesalat) 108

Contents
(Inhaltsverzeichnis)

Page / Seite

Minced Meat Salad
(Hackfleischsalat) 109

6 - Salad
(6 - Salat) 110

Herring Salad
(Heringsalat) 111

Salad Brabant Style
(Brabanter Salat) 112

Poultry Salad
(Geflügelsalat) 113

Raw Carrot and Apple Salad
(Möhren-Äpfel-Rohkost) 115

Pea Salad
(Erbsensalat) 116

Red Cabbage Salad
(Rotkohlsalat) 117

Desserts

Baked Peaches
(Gebackene Pfirsiche) 118

Gobbler's Laddies
(Schusterbuben) 119

Fried Elder-berry Blossoms
(Gebackene Holunderblüten) 120

Contents
(Inhaltsverzeichnis)

Page / Seite

Curd Broken Pancake
(Quarkschmarren) 121

Gentlemans Cream Pudding
(Herrencreme) 123

Cranberry Pudding
(Preiselbeerpudding) 124

Grapefruit Créme
(Grapefruit - Sahnecreme) 125

Witchs Créme
(Hexencreme) 126

Red Velvet Cream
(Rosa Samtspeise) 127

Egg Jelly
(Eiergelee) 128

Fruit Salad in Wine Jelly
(Obstsalat in Weingelee) 129

Ice-Cream Apples
(Gefüllte Eis-Äpfel) 130

Apricot "Negus"
(Aprikosen "Negus") 131

Rum Omelette
(Omelette mit Rum) 132

Contents
(Inhaltsverzeichnis)

Page / Seite

Chocolate Pancakes
(Schokoladen-Pfannkuchen)... 133

Cakes, Pies and Pastries

Hunters Cake
(Jägertorte)... 135

Cranberry Cake
(Schmand-Torte mit Preiselbeeren).. 137

Double Cream Cake
(Schmandkuchen).. 138

Pear Cake
(Birnentorte).. 139

Kiwi Cake
(Kiwi-Torte).. 141

Cream Cheese Raspberry Cake
(Käse - Sahne Torte mit Himbeeren).. 143

Gentlemans Cake
(Herrentorte).. 144

Prince Eugéne Cake
(Prinz - Eugen - Torte).. 145

Heavens Cake
(Himmelstorte)... 147

Apple Cake Westphalian Style
(Westfälischer Apfelkuchen)... 149

Contents
(Inhaltsverzeichnis)

Page / Seite

Brown Cherry Cake
(Brauner Kirschkuchen) 151

Cheese and Cherry Cake
(Kirschkäsekuchen) 152

Cheese Cake
(Käsekuchen) 154

Fruit Loaf - also known as Stollen
(Quarkstollen) 156

Terraced Cake
(Terassen-Kuchen) 158

Pineapple Cake
(Ananas-Kuchen) 160

Nut Cake
(Nußkuchen) 162

Gold and Silver
(Gold und Silber) 163

Red Wine Cake
(Rotweinkuchen) 164

Napoleon Cake
(Napoleon - Kuchen) 165

Banana Spicy Cake
(Bananen-Gewürzkuchen) 166

Contents
(Inhaltsverzeichnis)

Page / Seite

Banana Cake
(Bananenkuchen) 167

Pineapple Marzipan Cake
(Ananas-Marzipan-Kuchen) 168

Gooseberry Cake
(Stachelbeerkuchen) 169

Shaked Cake
(Schüttelkuchen) 170

Bio Cake
(Bio-Kuchen) 171

Potato Yeast Cake
(Kartoffelkuchen mit Hefe) 172

Pumpernickel Cake
(Pumpernickel-Kuchen) 173

Omnibus 175

Ballett Pieces
(Ballettschnitten) 176

Fine Waffles
(Feine Waffeln) 177

Curd Doughnuts
(Krübbelchen) 178

Carnaval Doughnuts
(Fastnachts-Krapfen) 179

Contents
(Inhaltsverzeichnis)

Page / Seite

Fried "Fragments"
(Badische Scherben) 180

Berlin Bread
(Berliner Brot) 182

Cold Dog's Muzzle
(Kalte Hundeschnauze) 183

Nürnberg Elise Gingerbread
(Nürnberger Elisen-Lebkuchen) 184

Rascals
(Spitzbuben) 186

Filled Oven-baked Doughnuts
(Kolatschen) 187

Nougat Crescent Rolls
(Nougat-Kipferln) 188

Salted Pretzels
(Salzbrezeln) 189

Holiday Favorites

Upper Palatinate Elder-Berry
(Oberpfälzer Hollerkoch) 190

Onion Pie / Swabia
(Zwiebelkuchen / Schwaben) 191

Black Forest Shovel
(Schwarzwälder Schäufele) 193

Contents
(Inhaltsverzeichnis)

Page / Seite

German Cheese Noodles
(Allgäuer Käs-Spätzle) 195

Emperors Broken Pancake / Austria
(Kaiserschmarrn / Österreich) 196

Steamed Dumplings / Alsace
(Dampfnudeln / Elsaß) 197

Chicken in Red Wine / France
(Coq au vin -Hahn in Rotwein / Frankreich) 199

Apple Cake / England
(Apfelkuchen / England) 201

Live Pâté / Denmark
(Leberpastete / Dänemark) 202

Danish Rolled Buns
(Hefeschnecken / Dänemark) 203

Whole Wheat Rolls / Danish "Boller"
(Grobe Weizenbrötchen / Dänische Boller) 204

Yugoslavian Moussaka
(Jugoslawischer Mussaka) 205

Güvetsch (Yugoslavia / Jugoslawien) 207